To J

MW01041304

Subre was my most prized gift & will be forever. Thank you, Wyndi Warren

Angel
With a Tail

By Wyndi Warren

Sabre Publishing Enterprise
Dallas, Texas, USA

ISBN-13: 978-1466334960
ISBN-10: 1466334967

Printed and bound in the United States of America by
CreateSpace
7290 B. Investment Drive
Charleston, SC 29418
USA

Edited by David W. Menefee

Sabre, my best friend. Photo courtesy of Fran Smith, Vancouver, BC.

Table of Contents

Acknowledgments

To adequately thank all those who have significantly contributed to this effort would probably require the writing of an additional book. There is only space to mention a few.

David W. Menefee returned a phone message. Our conversation sparked a series of events that turned a dream into something I could hold in my hands. His professional guidance, expertise, and extensive experience became the difference between a book and a forgotten file on my computer.

Ronnie, R.K. Mohr, D.V.M., was Sabre's angel and a friend to us both, through his caring and compassion for animals and the people who love them. The staff at Seagoville Veterinary Clinic will forever have my gratitude for their kindness and concern.

Marjorie Zimmerman, through her love, courage, and commitment to Jack Flash, created a vehicle for education and support of others who would share her experience of loss from Degenerative Myelopathy. Her website, established in 1998, has helped many to find rainbows within the storm.

Maria Werner devoted countless hours to reading each chapter and sharing invaluable comments and encouragement to help me tell the story of Sabre. Her constant support made this enterprise less daunting.

Leticia (Letty) Alamia, Ph.D., and Kathleen Conway, D.C., of Chaos Kennels hold ethical standards foremost through strict adherence and commitment to the German Shepherd breed and the welfare of their puppies. Because of them, I was privileged to have Sabre as my "dream dog."

Tamar, Linda, Maria, and all past moderators and members of the Degenerative Myelopathy Support Group were often the thin line between despair and hope during the early hours of my mornings.

A special thank you to Fran Smith for my treasured photos of Sabre.

One of my favorite quotations was written by Luciano De Crescenzo: "We are all angels with only one wing. We can only fly by embracing one another."

Through these and many other treasured friends, too many to name, the meaning of this quote lives forever in my heart.

Chapter 1
Pieces of a Dream

I know how foolish my words sound. I know some people would call me crazy, ridiculous, or maybe worse, but when the weather is cold, rainy, or hot enough to make even the trees sag in misery, I look up at the shelf in my living room to the cedar box that holds Sabre's ashes like a gift that can't be opened. Somehow, in some small way, I still feel that I'm keeping him safe.

Of course, I know the ashes are not Sabre, but I couldn't stand the thought, even imagined, that he could ever be wet and cold, or hungry, or miserable in the heat, buried in some lonely place that I can't reach. In my head, I know he's gone. In my heart, his spirit is no further away than my fingertips. His dark eyes look out from his picture on that shelf with that same fathomless wisdom I'd known for nine years.

The day he died, he was in perfect physical condition, except that he couldn't wag his tail. His strong, powerful back legs had wasted away until they could no longer hold his weight; they refused to move, lost to all feeling. His world, too, had wasted away until he could only drag himself from room to room.

Chapter 2
An Eighty-Pound Puppy

A summer day in Texas is only two degrees cooler than Hell. The air is humid and heavy, but, worst of all, a single August day is longer than the month of January and hardly the ideal weather to pick up your new German Shepherd puppy. Life has a way of giving the most wonderful presents in the worst imaginable wrappings.

As a kid, I fell in love with Bullet the Wonder Dog on black and white TV. I couldn't wait to get home from school to watch the latest episode, playing my sister's tennis racket like a guitar when Roy and Dale sang "Happy Trails." My six-year-old logic questioned the fairness of Lassie and Rin Tin Tin having shows of their own. Lassie swished her tail and did marvelous things, and Rin Tin Tin always came to the rescue, but Bullet was everything I wanted, the epitome of a German Shepherd dog. Bullet held me entranced as imagination painted him at my side, traveling in my child's eye to adventure and discovery. The years haven't erased those lyrics from my memory: "Happy trails to you until we meet again." I never imagined what those words would come to mean.

Growing up, my parents let me have dogs, mostly mixed breeds, strays that wandered onto our street. Although I dreamed of a German Shepherd, in their eyes a purebred dog cost money and the lost or abandoned dogs were free. Besides, they needed a home, too, and I loved them all. Sometimes I played with them to the exclusion of neighborhood friends and to my mother's consternation. But what do you expect from a kid who jumps off the roof just to see mom throw the laundry in the air?

My excitement bordered on uncontrollable that morning as I drove from Dallas to Grapevine, a tingling anticipation surging up inside me. The feeling was what I could only imagine would be like that of an Olympic athlete who knows the gold medal is about to be awarded, and not to someone else. I didn't notice the heat, brushing away beads of perspiration streaming down and burning my eyes. All I could focus on was a little voice in my head saying this German Shepherd would be the most special of all.

I arrived at EJ and Bob's kennel. The tires of my truck spawned whirlwinds of dust into the air, blocking out the view of Grapevine Lake a short distance away until the tiny particles settled sullenly back to the ground. Letty, whom I'd met before on several occasions, was unloading her dogs for a stopover after a dog show before the last leg home to south Texas. EJ and Bob had been friends of mine for over thirty years and ours was a unique relationship. EJ was part friend and part parent, while Bob was the handsome pilot whose warm smile could melt the coldest heart. In my younger days, when I really couldn't afford the price, EJ trusted me to pay her for my first German Shepherd puppies, $100 here, $50 there, until my name went on the line as owner on the registration papers. Without her, my childhood dream would not have come true for several more years.

Puppies were leaping out of the van and scattering in all directions as Letty herded them into the back yard. I didn't know which one would be going home with me. I walked to the fence and leaned across to watch the pack of gangly youngsters cavorting around the pool, sniffing, playing, glad to be out of the their crates after their long ride. Letty had told me about the dog she was bringing. He was nine months old, calm and sweet, intelligent and sound. She'd said his name was Tucker, but as Letty had described him on the phone, I knew his new name would be "Sabre."

My first assessment of these rowdy young pups produced no apparent candidate. I glanced at Sabre, but took him to be an older dog, possibly being groomed for bigger and better shows and I was surprised when Letty brought him over. He was handsome, black and glossy with deep red markings that picked up the rays of sunlight, shimmering in contrast to the midnight satin of his coat. His eyes, deep and brown, were older than his nine months. He greeted me politely, and then sat back as if there was nothing of interest to concern himself with. His attention wandered back to the pack of pups. I didn't attach any significance to his far away gaze at the time, but later wondered if, when he watched them, he had been thinking of the puppyhood he hadn't been allowed to live.

I didn't know Letty as well as I knew EJ, but like EJ, she didn't refuse to take puppies back when the owners couldn't keep them or no longer wanted them. She explained a little of his background.

"I sold him to a family in Louisiana, but they called about six months ago because he was just too much trouble," she shrugged, "so, I told them I'd take him back."

I assured her, "I like taking the older ones, less puddles to clean up."

He hadn't been abused; not in the ways you would normally think. The first few days after I got him home revealed the degree to which he had been ignored. The uncharacteristic detachment in his manner portrayed a doleful lack of enthusiasm. He was serious, studying me as I studied him. In all our time together, he would make me laugh more than anything or anyone I'd ever known.

After a short visit, I said my goodbyes. Without urging, he jumped into the back of my truck and settled onto the seat; no signs of excitement, nothing in his manner suggested that he was doing anything other than what he knew he was supposed to do.

Letty had told me she rotated him between friends so that he wouldn't become too attached to anyone until she could find a home for him. He calmly accepted this latest change, responsive but aloof. I stopped at the McDonald's for French fries and a burger. He followed my hand with his eyes, but made no attempt to close the distance from the back seat to the steaming food. I watched as, his curiosity apparently satisfied, he settled back against the seat. I offered him a French fry, which he gently took from my hand. As I drove off, he let his treat fall to the floor below. His gaze returned to the window.

I drove back to Dallas, thinking about what I'd seen, feeling a little like a taxi driver whose passenger was lost in thought. I'd expected him to gobble the French fry down, beg for more, and we'd be friends with the wave of a McDonald's French Fry Magic Wand. As I contemplated his unusual behavior, an idea came to me. I pulled off the road to an empty field, watching him out of the corner of my eye. Picking up the leash, I got out and opened the back door, slipping the clip into his collar. He obediently jumped to the ground. I led him into the field and stood still. He stood still, looking into the distance, not at me. I went forward. He went forward, still not looking up. I started to wonder if this was a dog, or a dog robot. I sat down under a scrubby little Texas tree, staring off at planes on the runway of DFW airport. He stood close, patiently waiting. I decided that I would remain still and quiet until he made the first move.

Minutes went by and nothing happened. Soon, his curiosity got the best of him; he lowered his head and sniffed in my direction. I reached up and placed my hand on his neck. He looked at me as if studying an odd apparition, then settled down beside me. I smiled and started to rub his head, his ears, and to talk to him until he rested his head on my leg. We stayed that way for a little longer; then I told him, "Lets go home."

We went upstairs upon arrival. The bowls for his food and water were in the kitchen on a dark blue mat embellished with a silhouette of Charlie Brown with his arm around his dog. I'd bought a purple ball that squeaked, a rope pull toy, and a rubber bone that I presented to him after giving him the chance to look around on his own. He looked at the ball and when I rolled it across the floor, he simply watched the strange object roll away. I showed him the pull toy and the rubber bone, but again got no reaction. He was nine months old and he didn't know what toys were. Saddened, I sat down on the floor pulling him to me, and promised him that I'd teach him how to play.

As we walked the grounds of the apartments later, I allowed him to stop to sniff, or go any direction he chose. I already knew he would follow wherever I led, so I decided he deserved the chance to explore. For the first time, I glimpsed a brief change in his demeanor, a tiny spark that let me know he enjoyed this gift of independence. In the days to come, he started to loosen up a little at a time, allowing his anticipation to show when I'd pick up his leash, knowing that time belonged to him.

And then, he discovered squirrels! They were everywhere, on the ground, in the trees. He looked up at me when one of them darted across his path, as if to ask permission, and I urged him to "Go git 'em!" My first mistake. This dog was unbelievably strong. I felt like Inspector Gadget being pulled from earth on a jet propelled rocket arm as he took off in a black, furry blur. I had no other choice at this point but to run behind or be pulled face first on the asphalt as we pursued the unfortunate little rodent that had wandered into Sabre's sights. In desperation, the imprudent pest jumped to the nearest tree. Sabre leaped against the trunk, trying to climb to the branches above him. I bent over gasping for breath and laughing at the same time. The squirrel, however, was outraged, maliciously chattering in Sabre's direction, and not sparing me from the disparaging squeaks. That was one mad squirrel, and one happy German Shepherd.

Our walks, three or four a day, became the high points of his daily routine, even better than dinnertime, although that was pretty good, too, especially when you consider the baked chicken livers added for extra flavor. One day, I saw a look in Sabre's eyes. He knew he finally owned a human. From that moment forward, he was a different dog than the one that had followed me up the stairs that hot August day.

Sabre at the Uptown apartment when I first got him. Photo courtesy of Fran Smith, Vancouver, BC.

One Sunday afternoon, the weather was perfect, the sky clear but for a few wistful clouds, and the air fresh, cooling with fall's promise of a break in the summer heat. We left the complex to stroll through the neighborhood. Sabre was his usual happy self, sniffing poles, leaving little messages for other dogs to follow, taking in new and wonderful smells along the way, but remaining vigilant for the marauding squirrel population. We walked for several blocks when I noticed cars slowing, people smiling and waving when I looked their way. I thought people were certainly friendly in this uptown part of the city. So, I smiled and waved back, with the satisfying knowledge that they were admiring my beautiful German Shepherd. I beamed with pride at everyone who noticed.

When we reached the gate, returning home, I happened to look down and discovered the reason for all the attention. Somewhere along the way, without my noticing, he had picked up a bright red pacifier, holding his acquisition firmly clenched in the side of his mouth. An eighty pound German Shepherd, with the size and mass to rip a small car apart, holding onto a baby's pacifier; I'd have slowed down, smiled, and waved, too.

As his newly discovered autonomy grew, Sabre invented his own version of a happy dance. With each departure from the apartment to go for a walk, he would stop in his tracks, throw his head to the left almost touching his tail, then throw his head to the right in the same arcing motion with equal gusto, then back to the left, and off we'd go in the direction of his choosing. Whenever he felt the urge, repeating this maneuver became his trademark expression of rapture.

Chapter 3

Revenge of the Deviant Squirrels

I quickly learned that with Sabre as my companion, there was no need to own an alarm clock. The moment he heard me start to stir, he was at my bedside, tail knocking against the armoire like a metronome. Sometimes I woke to him sitting silently beside the bed, waiting patiently for the start of a new day. If I failed to open more than one eye, he moved a little closer and breathed in my face. If that didn't get me up, he slammed his twenty-pound paw on the mattress and caused my pillow to reverberate like a clap of thunder rumbling its way across a stormy sky. I was fully alert by then. He was ecstatic. Job done, off he'd trot downstairs for his breakfast reward.

Sabre and I enjoyed our days together, while the deviant squirrels were plotting revenge. A large Sweet Gum tree grew just outside the breakfast nook of the apartment. The branches were within inches of the screened window. Pulling on my house shoes, I'd stumble down to the kitchen for my first cup of high octane coffee. Sabre followed for his anticipated Milk Bone.

The squirrels gathered in the tree. They sat there, these impudent, plume-tailed rats, twitching their tails, intent on creating havoc. If they had owned watches, they'd have been glancing at the time with glee. At just the right moment, they darted from branch to branch, hanging upside down on the trunk, cavorting from limb to limb. Chortling in that manner that only mad squirrels can, they teased and challenged us to come get them. These ill-mannered beasts from the dark side perceived that we couldn't do anything about their evil antics. They were safe beyond the glass panes of the window and made the most of their advantage.

At first, Sabre barked at them, not a good idea considering our early morning schedule. Then, he whined and bounced on his front legs, frustrated with the barrier holding him back. With each dawn, we awoke to a bevy of murderous squirrels, then made them run and climb for their lives as we made our rounds. Payback was the twenty-foot leash I bought to give Sabre the extra edge.

Evenings, however, were a sedate contrast to the early morning circus. Earlier in the week, I'd purchased an Eagles concert video. I've always liked their music and enjoyed playing along with my guitar, blissfully enjoying the fantasy that the group needed my help. I poured a glass of wine, lit a couple of candles, and settled on the couch in front of the television. Sabre was in his usual place beside the sliding doors to the patio. The candles flickered like the soft stirring of air when someone walks by, but I dismissed the idea, thinking the wavering was from the air conditioning cycling on and off. When I looked up, however, Sabre was sitting up with his head in between the vertical blinds. I thought he was watching traffic below until I noticed the erratic spurts of light on the other side. I laid my guitar on the couch and got up to look.

Outside, the weather was changing, and stark flashes of lightning slashed across a darkening sky. Sabre was enjoying the serenade and the light show. I pulled back the blinds, opened the doors, and joined him on the balcony. I'd forgotten my guitar, and the candles were snuffed out by the breeze. The Eagles played to an empty room. We became immersed in the exhilaration of the thunderstorm rolling through the city. Even as the first sprinkles of rain found their way to our faces, we watched the wind bend the trees into caricatures of skeletal gnomes lunging at the ground. Our enchantment grew as nature unleashed a majestic pageant of light, sound and fury. We watched the storm's finale, the day's fading hours slipping by until the sun slowly dipped into the river and the dusk melded into night. All that was left behind was the soft drone of rain.

Some dogs tremble in fear at the tempestuous cannonade; others don't notice the threatening disturbance. Sabre was enthralled. Whenever thunder pounded the sky, we were both drawn to the windows or doors. The lightning became an impromptu fireworks show sent solely for our enjoyment.

Without the advent of nature's more lively entertainment, days passed pleasantly on the six by four foot second floor balcony. Sabre soaked in the view of traffic below. He barked occasionally if someone walked by on the sidewalk outside the wrought iron fence. Accidents at our corner provided him with endless amusement, the equivalent of a widescreen television. He watched until the last vehicle rolled away. But his absolute delight was to hear another complex dweller, dog on leash, rounding his corner. His body would tense, much like a waiting panther, ready to spring. When the unsuspecting dog approached Sabre's designated zone, he exploded into action, barking and twirling, in full attack mode, causing the Shitzu, Maltese, or other unfortunate to shriek in terror, all four feet casting shadows on the pavement. More than once, I found myself leaning over the rail to apologize for my dog's regrettable lack of manners.

"I'm so sorry," I'd call out from the balcony, "he just gets so excited!"

Then, I'd slink back inside, with full knowledge that I wasn't sorry at all and laugh until tears rolled down my face. For Sabre, every night was Halloween and he was Chief Goblin in charge of wreaking havoc in the neighborhood.

His antics, however, came with a cost. Stucco is sharp, with knife-like edges surrounding each indentation and the crevices were plentiful and deep. This material, designed to resist the elements of weather, is as hard as concrete. The wrought iron railing provided an immovable opposing force, unbending when struck, immutable in the solitary purpose of keeping living things within narrow confines. Unfortunately, twenty four square feet of space didn't allow much room for spinning and twirling. Sabre was a powerful dog. He was solidly muscled in his shoulders as well as his haunches. With both ends whirling furiously, he was able to throw himself almost in a full circle, dropping back down only to turn and spin again.

As I closed the doors and blinds one night, I saw a drop of blood on the carpet. I turned the lights back on to examine Sabre, dismayed at finding the tip of his tail raw and bleeding. In striking the unforgiving surface, he had shaved the end of his tail. His skin was abraded, the hair missing for almost an inch. I took him upstairs and trimmed the remaining hair back to expose the wound. Carefully and gently, I soaked and cleansed his injury. Then, I wrapped the affected area with gauze and tape although I expected the bandage to be off when I awoke. Surprisingly, when I opened my eyes the next morning, he was still wearing his latest accessory like a kid with a new band-aid.

Three or four times a day, I repeated the cleansing process. He followed me upstairs willingly, never flinching at the warm salty water nor trying to pull away. His deep trusting eyes never left my face. After each session, he pranced away waving his bandage high, and I realized that Sabre enjoyed being a patient.

Depriving him of his nightly pursuit was difficult. Settled in his usual place, looking through the glass doors, he longed to go out on his patio. His disappointment was tangible. The next day, I went to the drug store and bought a metal finger splint, carefully taping the aluminum guard around his healing tail, padding the inside with cotton. His delight when I let him out that night surpassed that of a kid at Christmas. The phantom of the balcony was back! Each night when I brought him back in, I'd examine his tail for any signs of damage. Finding none, I concluded that his tail armor was effective and Sabre had his favorite pastime back again.

I became concerned that the healing process was taking too long. Although there were no signs of inflammation or infection, I decided to seek professional advice. I picked a vet in the area and took Sabre to be examined. Without unwrapping the bandage on his tail, the vet began what was apparently a practiced lecture.

"These injuries never heal correctly and the tip will

probably have to be amputated," he stated with authority.

I asked him, "Don't you want to look at it first?"

The look of surprise on his face was immediate, but he failed to recover fast enough to reply as I started to removing the tape. Sabre remained perfectly still while his tail was viewed from all directions.

Finally, the vet stood back from the table and said, "Whatever you're doing, keep it up."

I continued to soak and clean his tail, apply anti-bacterial ointment, and a brand new bandage each time. Eventually, his tail healed and the hair grew back around the bald end.

Unarguably, Sabre enjoyed every aspect of dressing up. He proudly displayed his vet-wrap adorned tail and beamed when I changed the color from red to blue to green. Each trip to the groomer for a new bandana around his neck prompted a happy dance on the way out the door. Maybe Sabre was bursting with pride that he owned a human who cared or maybe he just thought the colors blended nicely with his coat.

Chapter 4
The Stalker Cat

Sabre became my "go anywhere, do anything dog." Wherever I went, he went along. I remembered a statement Letty made in casual conversation, "He only wants to be with you."

Sabre was happy and content. I was more relaxed than I could remember being in a long time; even my blood pressure dropped from okay to "kick start my heart in the morning."

I enjoyed taking him with me to visit friends. One evening, we were invited to dinner at the home of one of my builders where I had just finished an outdoor project with a barbeque pit, a waterfall, and new plants along a flagstone path to the back yard. We were talking in the living room when the fattest Siamese cat I'd ever seen oozed into the room. Sabre's ears perked to attention, although he remained at my side, not attempting to rise. Pete's wife warned me that her cat loved to stalk and sometimes even attack unsuspecting dogs.

As we sipped our wine and talked, Stalker Cat got closer and closer, taking advantage of the limited view behind the corners of the furniture. Sabre started to get a little nervous when he didn't know exactly where the cat had gone. He got up once from his place on the floor but, I told him to lie back down. Reluctantly, he complied, but his stalker kept coming.

Finally, Sabre had enough. He stood, paying no attention to my admonishments, and in his loudest, fiercest bark, told Stalker Cat what I can only imagine was dog talk for exactly what he would do if the cat got any closer. His message got across. The cat disappeared, not to be seen again. Satisfied with his performance, Sabre returned to enjoying an evening with friends.

Chapter 5
Learning to Drive a Truck

The weeks rolled along at a lazy pace with work, going for walks, and enjoying an occasional television show before bedtime. Sabre, in his inimitable way, had obviously decided he was old enough now to learn to drive. I suspected he had an ulterior motive; there was a special golden retriever in the complex whose company he found most exhilarating.

Whenever I left him in the truck to run an errand, I came back out to find him firmly ensconced in the driver's seat. Nothing I tried could convince him that the seat was mine. Resigned to a battle I wasn't going to win, I bought a small brush to rid the seat and my clothes from dog hair decorations.

At the local Stop and Go one night, having made my purchase, I came out to find him sitting behind the wheel. A couple in the car next to us was laughing at the sight of my dog chauffeur, so I decided to play along. I slipped my extra key out of my pocket and walked around to the passenger's side. I unlocked the door, eased into the seat and started putting on the seat belt.

I was glad it was summer. If their faces had frozen with their looks of surprise, they'd have had to wear their expressions throughout the winter. I started to reach over and start the truck, but decided to end the game. That dog didn't need help with any more ideas.

Sabre had progressed from an aloof, contained, gentlemanly canine to something of a practical joker. His concept of humor corresponded with his sense of propriety. Some activities were only appropriate at certain times of the day with no exceptions. Milk Bones, for example, were for breakfast. They were not for munching in the middle of the day; afternoons were for chew sticks.

The first time I gave him a Milk Bone in the afternoon, temporarily out of his preferred delights, he let it drop to the floor. He looked up at me questioningly. No amount of assurance or urging could tempt him to do more than sniff. Reluctantly deciding that I wasn't going to give up, he took it and started walking around the apartment. The phone rang, and I lost track of him, but when I didn't see his treat anywhere concluded that the biscuit had been consumed.

At bedtime, I discovered the pillows on my bed in disarray. When I pulled the covers back, I found the Milk Bone, firmly nestled between the mattress and the headboard. He had tried to push the pillows back in place, but his housekeeping skills weren't adequately developed so he'd left them askew. I got the point.

He also considered it exceedingly rude of me to insist on answering my e-mail before preparing his dinner at night. Problem-solver that he'd become, he devised an ingenious way to interrupt my concentration.

First, he sat quietly by my side at the computer, leaning forward, lightly touching the hair on my arm with his chin. Then he slowly moved his head left, then right, and back again, without touching the skin. When I reached over to rub the itch, he poked his snout below my elbow and thrust his head up, simultaneously tossing my arm high in the air. Quicker than my eyes could follow, he slid the keyboard back under the desk with his nose where I couldn't reach it. I invariably started laughing, and when I looked back at the screen, whatever I was going to write was forgotten. With finesse and aplomb, Sabre had won another battle.

For all his calm, yet lighthearted demeanor, Sabre took his role as protector of the home very seriously. Without fail, the ringing doorbell would send him in a mad dash down the stairs to the front door, growling like a world class guard-dog. Each time I leaned out from the balcony rail, I saw most people involuntarily step away from the door. The ferocious sounds from within prompted a rapid retreat. The hardest I laughed was when the Dominoes Pizza ad came on the television and the chime in their commercial played. Sabre was up in a flash, tearing down the stairs, barking in his loudest voice. I didn't have the heart to tell him that the bell wasn't ours.

Excitement and fun was made up of squirrels and doorbells and the sound of a leash being taken from the shelf, but living in a small apartment has advantages and disadvantages. There's less space to clean, requiring less time, but additional tasks have to be added to the routine. Furry companions need to regular grooming, and Sabre was delighted to see his assortment of brushes come out of the drawer. With obvious excitement, off he bound to the balcony doors, urging me to move faster, and spinning in place until I pushed the door aside. In retrospect, I probably could have just stood still and held the brush in place. He'd have made all the necessary motions by moving against the bristles, then repeating in the opposing direction to fulfill his requirements.

The moments spent grooming made me feel closer to him than at any other time. There was a look of pure joy on his face, contentment in his eyes. Gone was the dignified aloofness, the quiet acceptance that life was life and not going to change. Gone was holding back love because there was no one who wanted his love. Sabre had learned to play. He owned a world of exploration, chasing squirrels, and going for rides in the truck. I hoped he'd forgotten his days of being ignored, and I believed he had when I studied the look in his eyes. He was happy, and frolic wasn't a collection of toys on the floor; play was everyday living and waking each day to do it all over again. Somewhere along the way, I'd come to feel exactly the same.

Chapter 6
The Gentleman German Shepherd

Life was not complete without ice cubes. We had an arrangement between us. When I'd pour a glass of water, filled with these frozen delicacies, I got the water and he got the ice cubes. Ice cube crunching parties were always a special occasion in winter or summer and in between. He crunched with enthusiasm, and then hunted for the little pieces he'd missed. If we went on a trip, I filled a plastic glass with ice cubes and fed them to him as we drove.

Being in the landscape business, I often thought I should have named my company "Have Shovel, Will Travel." One of my jobs took us almost to the Oklahoma border, to a small town on the edge of Lake Texoma. The reservoir is one of the more beautiful Corps of Engineer lakes that the state has to offer. Steep hills and intricate rock cliffs line its edges, and the silvery blue water stretches into the horizon even when viewed from high above. From the myriad assortment of trees, a bald eagle might soar within view, gracing the sky above. This trip was in the middle of winter on a cold inhospitable January day. The trees were stripped of their leaves, but the absence of foliage rendered the view open to the marvels below. The cold wind coming off of the lake brought tears to my eyes. With his lush double coat, Sabre hardly noticed. Although I wanted to stay in the truck with the heater, he was invigorated and wanted to run.

I'm not a champion of cold weather. I hate it. I tense up, I start to shiver, and then, I get grumpy. When my feet get cold, I have the charming disposition of an emotionally disturbed bear. Worse, I don't thaw out until July.

The house we'd gone to had been bought as a retirement

home, an unassuming structure with open spaces and a wrap around view of the lake across the back. The yard dropped off at the crest of a steep treed slope leading down to the water. The wooden dwelling was simple but engaging. Buffered by a circular drive, the front was set back from the road. Native rock stacked along the edges was joined to a long wooden ramp that invited visitors to the door. Sabre had launched himself from the back seat when I opened his door, running before his feet even hit the ground. I stood shivering, missing the warmth of the truck. After a few minutes, I called him and headed up the walkway. He fell in behind. Whatever I asked of him, Sabre did without reluctance or hesitation; he was happy to go along.

When we reached the half-way point of the walkway, a panicked cottontail rabbit jumped out from under the boardwalk and streaked across the yard, desperate to escape. Sabre looked up and whimpered. I told him, "Go!" However, being the Uptown gentleman that he was, did he leap over the rails or try to wedge through? No. He went back to the beginning of the ramp, and then lurched across the yard in pursuit of the rabbit. Unfortunately, by the time he got back to the driveway, the rabbit was two counties away, but I let him track the hapless bunny anyway. Sabre frantically searched the yard, making me laugh until my sides hurt. I forgot all about being cold.

When we got home later, we were tired, but I still had e-mails to answer. Sabre kept putting his nose under my arm, snuggling and blocking the keyboard. I thought he just wanted show his gratitude for the day. I stopped to pet him, thinking that would suffice, but he evidently wanted me to stop with no intention of being denied.

In my clever human mind, I decided that in order to complete my tasks with fewer interruptions, I'd supply his favorite treat. Instead of just giving him one ice cube, then having to stop and wipe my hand with a towel, I decided to put three or four on the floor in front of him hoping that would buy extra time. I returned to the computer believing the problem was solved.

As I muddled through my correspondence, I became aware of sounds that had nothing to do with crunching ice cubes. I stopped to watch. Saber, in his own clever way, was chomping the first ice cube, and then running up and down the stairs, hiding the others behind the tables, the curtains, or the couch in the living room. He tucked them into the corners for enjoyment later at his leisure. I was treated to an indoor Easter egg hunt, but for ice cubes instead of colored eggs. Sabre didn't realize that his little treasures would only melt away to nothing and was probably dismayed at seeing me collect and deposit them in the sink. But, as with everything, he was forgiving, apparently secure in his knowledge that I would not purposefully cause him displeasure or harm.

Sabre loved listening to music.

Chapter 7
"Precious" is a Donkey

A midweek telephone call brought a pleasant surprise a couple of weeks later. A friend was coming to Dallas for a business trip. My apartment seemed the logical place for her to stay, so I extended the invitation and told Sabre, "We're gonna have a house guest!" He listened intently, that serious, but accepting look on his face. Sabre was always ready for the next adventure, but, of course, he knew that people didn't come to visit me, they came to see him. He diligently monitored preparations, supervising to insure that the groceries went into the right places and noting that the cleaning process was thorough and correct.

He wasn't happy that we went out to eat the first evening, and I glanced up at him sitting behind the glass doors of the balcony as we drove off with a tinge of guilt. When we returned he greeted us with his twitching nose, leading us up the stairs, gracious host that he was. He had no complaints with sharing his home with our guest and quickly assumed his hosting duties.

After the lights went out and I had settled into bed upstairs, I heard laughter from below. I listened for a moment, and then called down to ask what was so funny.

My guest giggled, "Your dog is sitting here staring me in the face. It's like he's asking, what are you doing on my couch?"

This was our first overnight company, but not the first time Sabre's expressions were interpreted as closely aligned with those of humans. In that instance, Sabre was obviously fascinated by the experience and determined to explore every aspect.

Although he reveled in the guests we invited, he also enjoyed trips to visit friends. A friend had moved an hour's drive from the city. On a Sunday afternoon, we hopped into the truck for a day in the country. Along the way, Sabre and I had our first spat.

The day wasn't warm, but it wasn't cold either, vacillating somewhere in between. It was one of those days that fluctuated between making the decision to turn on the heater or to flip the air conditioning switch. Sabre had a marked preference for the air conditioning. At first I thought his panting in my ear meant he needed to stop for exercise, but that didn't seem to be the issue. We got back on the road. He settled back against the seat, but was soon sitting over the console panting in my ear again. I guessed I had turned the heater on without his approval. I turned it off and cracked the window; he returned to watching the landscape roll by. Soon, my feet started to chill, and I turned the heater back on. I would almost swear that he raised an eye at my thoughtlessness and he was immediately back to breathing in my ear. This process repeated for the next thirty miles until we finally reached our destination.

All was forgiven when we pulled into the drive. Sabre hopped from the truck to the smells of the countryside, with numerous dogs, cats, and horses, and a Sicilian donkey named "Precious." Sabre was enthralled with this large creature that sported foot long ears and a thin, swishing tail. He made his way to the fence, pushing his nose through the wire as Precious leaned down to investigate the new critter on her turf.

Donkeys are kept with horses because they are the defenders of their pasture. A Sicilian donkey is twice the size of a domestic cousin, but with more personality and a discerning intelligence. Their innate urge to protect is especially valuable when there are foals. The mother is able to get their young to safety while their protector takes on the invader. Stray dogs, wolves, or coyotes breach the boundaries at their own risk. A donkey will fiercely protect its charges, and is quite capable of chasing off or stomping to death any beast foolish enough to enter any designated domain. We all watched to see if Precious would regard Sabre as friend or foe.

After studying each other carefully, Precious leaned closer, within reach of Sabre's nose. I cringed, wondering if she wanted to bite it off. She stood there staring down at him, apparently sensing no danger, and graciously accepted Sabre's kisses. We knew then he had passed her test. What Precious didn't realize was that Sabre had added another charm to his bracelet with her name engraved.

Back home, Sabre was one tired pup. He ate his dinner, forsaking his usual balcony vigil, and fell asleep by the patio doors, dreaming of horses and pastures and adoring donkeys.

Another memorable venture was a camping trip at the border of the Texas and Oklahoma state lines. My closest friends had recently purchased a large travel trailer to replace the pop-up they had used and not yet sold. They brought the pop-up along for Sabre and me. Having watched the preparations and assembly of camping gear, Sabre's ears perked up when I started to carry our equipment down to the truck. No urging was needed for him to leap into the back for the ride to wherever we were going. A surprise, however, awaited my noble companion when we arrived.

We set out early; I was anxious to get on the road ahead of holiday traffic. I had filled the large plastic travel cup with ice cubes and water and placed it in the console beside my seat. We cruised along, enjoying the sights that streamed by outside of the windows. Stands of native trees, in varying shades of green, contrasted against the fathomless azure of the surrounding sky, stretching out over the miles. The rhythm of travel was soothing and pleasant.

Road trips always included a supply of CDs I'd compiled with music that radio stations rarely played. The old tunes had a way of bringing memories of places and people long past. These thoughts brought forward the echoes of dreams fulfilled and the ones left behind. I could play one song over and over, and Sabre never complained like most human companions.

When I reached down for a sip of water, I noticed that the volume of water had diminished considerably, but I knew I hadn't drunk that much. So, I started to watch out of the corner of my eye as I drove. Sabre was clever. He'd reasoned that getting the ice cubes from the glass didn't have a strong probability for success, so he settled for the water instead. However, he apparently didn't want me to discover his slippery maneuvering, so he edged over the console and kissed my ear to distract me with affection. Then, when my eyes were firmly on the road, he took a drink. I laughed and picked up the glass, tipping it in his direction, in an unspoken agreement between friends. He drank happily and to show his further gratitude, kissed my ear with a tongue so cold that I shivered.

We arrived at the campsite, anticipating a welcomed respite from life in the city. Sabre greeted Marty and Gloria exuberantly, but stopped in his tracks when he spied two furry black blobs quaking behind their legs. No amount of urging could get these furry pups to forsake their imagined safety barriers and face the huge beast that had suddenly appeared in their midst. They were convinced they were about to be eaten alive.

I had been repeatedly awed at Sabre's ability to sense the feelings of humans and other beings he encountered. He possessed a calm serenity that offered no threat, engendered no fear beyond the shock of his size. He seemed aware of their angst, as he stood quietly until their initial alarm dissipated. Lowering himself to the ground lessened the difference and further quelled their fright. One after the other, the pups tentatively peered out from their hiding place as curiosity took over. Sabre was gentle, softly sniffing each in turn and allowing them to explore the huge apparition that had descended into their midst. Soon, they were frolicking around, enchanted by their new friend.

Holly and Candy were from the same litter of standard poodles, solid black and adorable. Born with one ear undeveloped, Candy was more reticent than her sister Holly, usually hanging back while her litter mate took the lead. Jubilant in her exploration, Holly leaped on Sabre's back, sliding off in a tangle of feet and ears, tumbling to the ground and promptly getting back up to do it again and again. Candy was soon at her heels. Sabre patiently tolerated all their antics, sharing their fun, and finding amusement in their clumsy playfulness. We watched them, enthralled and fascinated that the difference in their sizes had no bearing on the quality of their play.

Holly was delighted with her new toy, but Candy was smitten, and sometime during the weekend, she began a lifetime of infatuation with the handsome, self-assured German Shepherd that had come into her life. Saber immediately claimed them both as members of his pack.

Chapter 8
Christmas is for Dogs

Our last Christmas in the apartment marked the beginning of a new phase of entertainment. For the first time, we went out to look at Christmas lights. Several times, I'd taken him for rides in the busier areas of the local nightlife. He soaked up the sounds and watched intently as people moved about on the sidewalks and streets, taking it all in. The next obvious choice was to enjoy Christmas decorations. Any scene we found that had moving parts and music playing was a hit with him. His attention never wandered, and even as we drove away, his gaze shifted forward, anticipating the next one.

The point is frequently made that dogs can't distinguish colors. That didn't seem to fit for Sabre; he always seemed to home in on a particular part of a display. His demeanor changed; his stance adjusted as if to study the object in his view. He thrust his head forward, ears tuned in a definable direction. Many times, I wondered aloud, "Just what do you see?" He glanced up briefly, returning immediately to whatever riveted his attention, committed to the sights and sounds. While my eyes were drawn to reds and whites, his seemed to follow the softer colors. I contemplated the direction of his gaze, expecting him to be studying the most active parts of the display. However, he seemed to be drawn to the blue and the green ones. Whether the displays were static or moving made no difference. His eyes moved if the lights did not. I became more interested in watching him.

I had never doubted that Sabre did, in fact, think and reason. Observation alone of the choices he made and the things he did left no question. His behavior was purposeful, deliberate, and infused with logic incredibly similar to that of human beings.

I'd read reports in magazines, newspapers, or on the internet that dogs don't see red very well, but blues and greens are within their ability to distinguish. At that time, I was operating under the assumption that they could only ascertain light and dark, black, white, and gray, basing most of their pursuits on instinct or sensing motion. His attention to static parts of the displays defied that logic.

Sabre wasn't left out of the festivities of the Christmas season. At home, a brightly wrapped present was waiting with his name on the tag. I rationalized that, since dogs don't follow a calendar and could care less what name was assigned to a day, there was no reason to wait until Christmas. Allowing him to open his gift for himself, however, would have been so out of character for Sabre as to have been impossible. That would have meant tearing something up, and Sabre did not do that, not to anything. I'd been told he was one of the puppies in what Letty called the "Mess with it Litter." These pups shared a proclivity for picking things up and moving them, but never tried to destroy chosen objects. They clearly had a flair for rearranging.

I ripped off the paper and the ribbons for him. Inside was a stuffed toy, a velvety, black dog, with long floppy ears and protruding nose, positioned upright with the tail tucked behind. When presented with his new treasure, Sabre gratefully accepted his gift, firmly grasped in his mouth, then gingerly placed the curious favor on the floor. He sat back and stared down expectantly. First, he sniffed, and then he nudged the head and middle with his nose, but neither act brought any response. I watched in fascination when he picked it up and started to wander throughout the apartment, often coming back to where he started, and then walking around again. His motive soon became clear. He was looking for a place that was secure from harm. He finally found a corner of the living room where his toy wouldn't be stepped on, but with the added benefit of a clear view of the balcony. Whenever relocation became necessary for vacuuming or other reasons, Sabre came quickly to the rescue, moving the cloth replica now known as "Baby" to another safe haven where it remained under his watchful eye. I no longer bought balls, pull ropes, or rubber bones. I sought out stuffed toys in the form of ducks that quacked, gorillas that laughed, or funny little dogs that barked. They became his litter, and I was convinced he'd been a mother dog in a former life. Although he placed them gently in out of the way corners or sometimes between the pillows on the couch, he frequently decided they had been in one place too long and needed a change of scenery. He took them outside to enjoy the view, tucked between his front paws. He remembered to bring them back inside. He became especially wary when someone came into the apartment, and he wouldn't leave his precious charges anywhere if he was being watched. They were his litter of make-believe puppies and he took his responsibility seriously.

That particular Christmas, I realized that Sabre needed a back yard, where he could lie out in the sun in cool weather and chase squirrels without a leash. He had also made it clear, invariably whimpering from the back seat of the truck when anyone walked by with their dog, that along with having a home and his own human, he wanted a special companion. He loved people, but "four-leggeds" needed the company of other "four-leggeds." There was no space in our small confines for another German Shepherd, and Sabre wanted a puppy. Although I had fully enjoyed the relative freedom of calling the apartment office if anything went wrong, I concluded the time had come to look for a house. My search began in earnest.

That sense of urgency amplified when Sabre developed what appeared to be a fungus on the tip of his ears. He had begun to scratch at his ears, and I first thought they were dirty. I pulled out the cotton balls and Q-tips thinking a thorough cleaning would solve the problem.

The next few days brought no apparent relief; he still scratched furiously. When I examined his ears again, I noticed that tiny tufts of hair were wafting off the ends, leaving bare skin exposed. The only thing to do was to take him to the vet. I'd had him groomed at a vet's office a few blocks away and returned. Sabre had great fun eying all the other dogs and thought the cats lying around on the counters were quite a nice touch to the decor. No boring magazines or staring into space for him. His exuberance dictated that I wouldn't be reading the magazines, either.

We were finally admitted to one of the examination rooms and waited patiently for the vet to appear. Our vet of the day didn't seem to know exactly what was wrong, but prescribed an ear wash and ointment to rub on the affected areas several times a day. I followed the instructions, and Sabre, as usual, made the most of the doctor-patient game. However, his ears did not show any improvement when the medication was close to running out. I took him back. The next vet we saw offered another solution. We went home with a different treatment. Still, there was no improvement. In fact, the problem was getting worse. I became frustrated at this point because no one seemed to be able to make a firm diagnosis, vaguely alluding to a "fungus."

Sabre was becoming more miserable with the passing days. On our last visit, the third vet commented that she'd been seeing more dogs with the same malady. I started thinking that none of the dogs we saw on a regular basis, visiting or on his daily walks, had displayed any symptoms like his. The only other place we had been was this vet office for grooming. The obvious decision at that point was to go somewhere else, but all the city vets seemed to operate on the same principle of rotating personnel. I called my friend Trudy for suggestions.

On the referral of Trudy and her sister Nancy, Sabre and I found Ronnie. After calling for an appointment, my itchy companion and I set out for a small town on the outskirts of Dallas called Seagoville. The municipality had once been the site of an interment camp for German, Italian, and Japanese prisoners during World War II. The facility was now a federal prison. Although Ronnie's clinic was about thirty minutes from downtown Dallas, the drive proved to be worth every mile.

Ronnie greeted Sabre, and Sabre was immediately responsive. I'd learned that my dog was a much better judge of character than me, so I relied on his good judgment. This tall, home-grown vet was the epitome of a country doctor for people, except that he treated and cared for animals along with the people who loved them. Having grown up in a small town, his manner was easy and gentle, yet exceedingly thorough. He talked to Sabre, appearing to pet him more than examine him. I watched and appreciatively listened to the thoughts he expressed out loud. He prescribed a liquid to be applied three times a day and asked that I call him back in a couple of days. Within the first day, Sabre seemed less concerned with his ears. To my untrained eye, the medicine was working. I knew we'd found our vet. I tried to suppress my anger at all the time wasted and the discomfort Sabre had suffered. Although his ears healed in a matter of a couple of weeks, the scars never diminished. I told him, "Don't worry, Sabre; it gives you character." He seemed to like the idea.

Winter soon arrived bringing a fluctuating pattern of snow and ice that only Texas can bestow without mercy on its inhabitants. The uncertainty of weather impeded the search for our new dwelling. Although most winters are relatively devoid of snow or ice, sometimes the months of January and February are accorded both. Variations can range from piercingly cold and clear to rainy episodes that tingle with the threat of sleet. Occasionally, the days are balmy respites where one only needs a light jacket to be comfortable.

One Sunday morning, we awoke to a silent barrage of white fluffy flakes dancing across the windows and drifting onto the ground below. Since snow isn't a predominant occurrence in the local climate, when it does happen, people celebrate and spirits lift, striking a remnant joy of childhood even in the most jaded adults. This snowfall was like a phantom that filled the air, the still green grass fading softly to speckled white, yet a glance at the streets and sidewalks showed no evidence of its presence, other than rendering the concrete shiny from the melted wetness.

Sabre and I were captivated by the view outside, mesmerized by the motion of the whispering whiteness pirouetting to the ground. The world beyond was a fairytale vision of tranquility and grace, alien to the normal hustle and bustle of life in the city. I poured my cup of coffee, carried it over to the fireplace, and sat down. Time seemed to float along with the snow, owning no importance or consequence in the moments that Sabre and I lingered side by side, absorbed in the quietude.

The wet flakes continued throughout the day, punctuating our walks with a touch of excitement and novelty that Sabre found intriguing. Head turned sideways, his eyes crossing at flakes settling on the top of his nose, he'd look up at me as if wondering how I'd arranged this unusual phenomenon to spice up his daily excursions. Sabre never failed to show gratitude even for the simplest things, a tasty dinner, and jaunts around the complex beleaguering the impertinent squirrels, or wandering over a job site while I conducted business. No gift was ever too small for him to acclaim.

The next blast of weather turned rogue was an arctic system that draped the city in a sheath of ice three or four inches thick. The parking lot became an ice skating rink, beckoning every kid in the complex to slip and slide across the winter playground.

Sabre's four legs clearly gave him the advantage of balance. I slipped the lead off his collar, watching as he frolicked with the kids on the ice. A younger boy stood off to the side. At first, I thought he might be afraid of getting hurt, but a closer study of his expression said something entirely different. His was the pain of not fitting in, coupled with the impression that exclusion was a familiar plight. Not trying to join was preferable to being rejected. Sabre must have sensed it, too.

I watched as he slowly approached and the youngster tentatively reached out to pet his head. Sabre may not have been able to form human words, but his nose spoke clearly enough for him. He nudged the boy, licking his gloved hand, and slipping up under his arm. Moments later, Sabre had become the locomotive and the boy was his train. With my giant German Shepherd navigating the ice, the boy holding on to his collar and back, they cavorted around the rest. Soon, the others stopped to watch and started cheering and urging them on. The laughter made me smile. At the same time, I reached up to wipe a tear from my eye before it could freeze on my face. Sabre had touched yet another heart.

One of our favorite activities was to visit the pet store. Sabre was delighted to help with the shopping. Carefully examining items on the shelves, he appeared to be reading the labels. My eyes wandered to another dog sharing the aisle. I found myself staring and quickly turned away. A striking tri-color Corgi struggled to keep up with his owner. I couldn't determine whether the disfigured back leg was the result of disease or an injury. I glanced back to Sabre, his noble stance and regal bearing causing my heart to flutter with pride. Coat shining, eyes sparkling, he was the picture of perfect health. I vowed that I would never allow anything bad to happen to him.

Chapter 9

Buy Me a House, Please

I revived the search for a new home, usually going out weekend afternoons or on the way home from work. I looked at condos, but none seemed to have enough space to roam, and Sabre would have been limited to walking any distance away on his leash. Eliminating the busier parts of town, I targeted an area referred to as Old East Dallas that offered small, medium, and large-sized homes with mature trees, eclectic people, and, of course, a significant squirrel population. I wanted a place where we could walk in relative safety, without busy thoroughfares, but also having open spaces where I could take the leash off and allow Sabre to run free. The endeavor continued for just short of two years.

I found the most honest realtor Dallas had to offer. Personable, patient, and sincere, Marsue never gave up. We had inspected a dwelling a few blocks away, one of many houses we had toured, but the residence would have needed a carpenter in full-time residence.

Almost by accident, we found a house that was perfect. On the way back to where we'd started, Marsue said, "I just happened to think of another house you might want to look at."

A short drive brought us to an unassuming structure with paned windows on each side of the entry. Large trees framed the front. The charming home was encased in light colored brick with a sea of green grass and Asian jasmine providing a backdrop. I knew instantly that the trees would attract a never ending supply of pesky squirrels.

From the moment I walked through the door, the decision was obvious. The kitchen was a little large since all my cooking ability allows for is meals that only have three ingredients and take five minutes to prepare. The breakfast nook with its wrap around windows prompted visions of morning coffee and leisurely dining. The view across the street encompassed a park-like triangle of grass with Pecan trees and crepe myrtles that served to obscure the traffic beyond. An amusing coincidence was that Marsue lived right across the street.

I wondered if Sabre might miss his widescreen TV and his favorite reality shows, Rush Hour and Traffic Accident. At the apartment, there was almost constant activity on the street below, enhanced by other residents coming and going. This street seemed almost too quiet.

My fears were soon assuaged when I learned that the house claimed one of the primary routes for kids going to school and coming back home. With an elementary school and a high school nearby, there would be plenty of sights and sounds to keep him entertained. The best part was six tall windows in the breakfast room at the precise height for a German Shepherd taking in the sights. Peacefulness in this world is in short supply, yet peace and solitude were exactly what I found in that laid-back neighborhood.

When my offer on the house, which was just the right size or maybe a little larger than I wanted, was accepted, I was fortunate.

Sabre immediately distinguished the differences between the apartment and our new home. He settled in right away, claiming the coziest nooks for a nap. He found vantage points with entrances and exits visible at the same time. I'd walk in the kitchen to see him lying at the windows, resting his chin on the window sills, thoughtfully situated ten inches above the floor.

The patio had been converted into an office. The arbor outside the door was adorned each summer with the striking orange flowers of trumpet vines winding around four posts and stretching over the top. A fat, green hummingbird appeared almost daily to sample the nectar of the blossoms. Blue Jays, Robins, Cardinals, Mourning Doves, and a number of other species called the huge oak trees home. Squirrels were abundant and equal in impudence to the ones at the apartment; Sabre never had to worry about something to chase.

A few nights after we moved in, I questioned my decision. I was preparing for bed when I heard a noise that I knew was a gun shot, followed by the screech of metal on concrete, the unmistakable cacophony of automobiles crashing into each other. I quickly put my clothes back on and went outside. At the corner of the street, one car had landed on its roof and an SUV had plowed into the crepe myrtles on the median.

A young man dicd that night over an imagined or inadvertent insult at a near-by boxing club. He was lying over the edge of the back seat of the SUV when I walked up; he was struggling for breath, moaning the way unconscious souls do, unaware of the reality of the horrible scene surrounding him. The air smelled of metallic steam, hot oil, and worse, there was no breeze. The odors of devastation sank slowly to the ground, smothering grass and pavement alike, settling on the shoulders of those nearby.

I moved closer when I saw that he was slipping out of the vehicle. Inching toward a four foot drop, he would have landed on his head and likely have broken his neck. I yelled at two men on the sidewalk, "Help me! He's falling out."

They hurried over. Together, arms underneath his shoulders, we supported his weight, staying the inevitable fall. These two strangers and I remained in position until help arrived. I noticed when a police officer picked up a pistol that was probably thrown from the car along with the passengers. I studied those involved in the wreck. They were kids, not nearly as tough now as I'm sure they felt before one fired the shot, and both drivers lost control. My eyes followed the progress of the stretcher to the ambulance where a sheet was pulled over his face.

Saddened, I walked back home. Sabre followed me through

the house like a shadow, watching closely, but not crowding me. He approached slowly when I sat down, calm and sure, like a good friend who doesn't have to ask what's wrong. I held him for a while without talking, stroking his soft ears, feeling him breathe beside me. His dark eyes were reassuring and his presence conveyed a strength reaching far beyond human ability. Sabre was my fortress against the hurts of the world. I wondered if the young men involved in the night's tragedy had known the kind of love and devotion he freely gave, would they have been so quick to grasp at violence to even a score?

Several minutes passed before I was able to calm the dark aura that hovered over me. After holding Sabre and a quick shower, I slept soundly, freed from the residual uneasiness from the sights and sounds of the night's tragedy.

Chapter 10
The Poltergeist

The days followed with no other incidents. I soon lost the feelings of apprehension, but the strangest incidents were happening right inside the house. I'm something of a creature of habit in a lot of ways, and totally unpredictable in others. A friend tells me I'm a "walking contradiction." However, most of my routines have to do with work. At the end of the day, I pull everything out of my pockets, put them on the table by the computer, check e-mail, and then head for the shower. The next morning, I pour my coffee, check e-mails, shower, load up my pockets, and head for the door.

As regular as my routine was, my keys and my billfold kept disappearing from where I put them. I'd get ready to leave and not be able to find either or both. My frustration was dampened slightly with the recurring events because I thought the culprit might be my "mess with it dog" at work. Although I could see him snagging my billfold, picking up my keys didn't fit the scenario. His choices were usually targets of opportunity and not apt to catch his notice more than once. I noticed, however, a subtle restlessness in Sabre's demeanor. He seemed more alert than usual, lifting his head frequently as if hearing noises, although I never heard anything aside from traffic or an occasional voice from the street. He also often looked up from his dinner, as if someone had entered the room, but, no one was there.

Occasionally during the night, I awoke to him wandering through my bedroom to the windows and then back out to the rest of the house for no reason I could determine. The times I got up to look, there was nothing amiss. All the while, once or twice a week, my keys or my billfold were missing. Sometimes, I left the office to look elsewhere in the house, and when I came back, the missing article was back in place. I guess any normal person would have concluded that they were loosing their faculties, and I have to admit the same thought did enter my mind. I could not find any reason for what was occurring

My irritation was mounting, especially one morning when I was late for an appointment and the keys were not where I knew I'd left them. I had two sets of keys; the set I usually used had been missing for a couple of days and now the second set was gone. I turned to Sabre and confronted him, demanding that he stop what he was doing. The look on his face immediately erased any doubt. His head sank low between his shoulders, his tail wagging slowly behind him, as he crumbled under my judgment. Logic told me that the probability of Sabre taking the keys, then putting them back beside the printer was extremely low, but emotion can sometimes override sensibility. I was immediately ashamed. I dropped to my knees in front of him, apologizing for my false accusation. I hugged his neck and stroked his head. I knew that he had nothing to do with the strange disappearances. I called my client, explaining I'd be late and searched the office again, but with no success. I sat down on the couch in the living room, Sabre by my side, perplexed, wondering what to do next.

I rose to look again, and I found the keys back beside the printer. I was completely baffled and even Sabre seemed unnerved. He was determined to go with me when I started to leave, pushing himself through the doorway. I sensed his distress and relented. He leaped into the truck and sat up staring at the house until we drove away.

My guilt didn't lessen when we returned to the house. I took Sabre out to the back yard and brushed him, still apologizing. I went back to my office, searching everything on top of the table and by the printer. My efforts were futile. The other set of keys was nowhere to be found and I was out of answers. Turning to Sabre, I told him, "Lets go," and we headed for the hardware store.

While he patiently waited, I had three new sets of keys made. One set was stored by the printer, one in the living room, and one in my bedroom. The next morning, the set by the printer was gone!

I started taking Sabre with me every day, everywhere I went, even if it was only a quick walk two houses away to talk to a neighbor. I didn't want to leave him alone in the house.

One evening, the phone rang. Trudy, a friend of many years, was on the other end. I mentioned the strange happenings that I had laughed off as creeping senior moments or early Alzheimer's syndrome, but she took the serious side of the issue.

"A poltergeist, maybe," she offered, exploring the possibilities. She suggested a Native American ritual that her sister Nancy practiced. I agreed to have Nancy come and smudge the house. I always enjoyed their visits, and I was open to any solution that could relieve my dilemma. I reasoned that no harm could come from trying and the date was set.

Sabre greeted his guests excitedly, making certain each got equal affection. He distributed his kisses judiciously; his delight at seeing the humans who belonged to Precious come through his door was obvious and genuine. Cups of coffee were placed on the table as we sat down to talk. Sabre settled at our feet, patiently looking out his windows, tuning out our chatter. He was accustomed to this strange human convention.

Nancy assembled the needed articles and soon we got up to begin. Sabre perked up, tail wagging in measured beats. His keen eyes were drawn to the flash of the match, the tendrils of smoke rising from the sage in the shell. The fire was captured deep within; no flames were seen. We walked slowly from room to room, allowing the smoke from the burning sage to permeate even the smallest crevices. Nancy explained that if any unwanted spirit was present, through the blessings of the sage, the entity would have no choice but to do as directed and leave. Sabre stayed close, his attention on the billowing smoke, sometimes reaching the corners of the rooms before us. Nancy repeated the chant that gave the ritual power, waving the smoke in all directions with her hand. She had warned that if any presence was encountered, the sage would burst into flame, rising up in the exhortation to immediately leave and never return.

Her softly spoken chant had the effect of lulling the participants into a sense of inner concentration and focus. We moved from the kitchen to the living room, the front bedroom, the shower, and the dressing area, with Sabre quietly beside us. When she opened the door to the large closet in my bedroom, the flame suddenly spewed a foot in the air.

Nancy yelled, "Open the window! Open the window!"

I quickly threw open the window above the toilet as she followed with the shell. The leaping flame once again receded to a low whispering of smoke as I closed it back again. I glanced over at Nancy.

From the burnished tan of the East Texas sun, her face had paled to a banker's pall. She said, in a trembling voice, "It's gone."

After a moment, our composure regained, we finished the remaining rooms of the house. She then turned to Sabre, gently moving the smoke from the shell in his direction. He didn't move. He sat in front of her, his eyes following her waving hand.

The calmness that befell our little group, Sabre included, and the lighter atmosphere of the house could be felt at some primal level and lasted into the following days. Sabre no longer seemed overly alert. I felt relaxed, and my keys and billfold stopped disappearing. Belief, I suppose, is in the eye of the believer, but the ambiance of the house was unquestionably changed, although I never again found the first set of keys.

Chapter 11

I Don't Want to Share!

A few months later, we discovered his favorite Christmas house only three blocks from ours. Decorations dangled in every available space, Christmas carols played in the background, and lights of all colors hung from the trees in masses of single-hued brilliance that twinkled in the grass and on the roof. Windows and doors were framed in beckoning contrast. There was no choice other than to park in front, kill the engine, and watch and listen.

The time had come to fulfill another promise to Sabre. All he ever wanted was a home, his own human, and a puppy. He had a home and he had a human, but there were two problems to solve before fulfilling his last desire. The fence in back bordered the driveway from the alley to the garage, effectively dividing the backyard into halves. I installed a sliding gate across the back and discarded the dividing portion of the fence. With the change, Sabre had full run from corner to corner and enough space for two German Shepherds to play.

The fence was the easier problem; the more difficult struggle was in me. I wasn't convinced I could love another dog the same way that I loved him. Sabre was like no other; he was part of me, as essential to living as being able to breathe.

Each time that someone walked by with their dog, Sabre whimpered and strained to get as close as he could. His desperation burst through as he pulled against his leash, the yearning in him so strong as to blot out everything else around him. I could no longer ignore the message he unwaveringly conveyed. A promise is a promise, so I knew I had to help him find his puppy.

No one I knew had a suitable candidate. I'd always been willing to take the older dogs that had been returned when people moved and were unable to take them along, or those who came back because they could no longer be cared for. EJ, at the time, had no prospects. Letty only had males. I widened my search.

Many phone calls and emails later, I had lined up two prospects. The first puppy we went to see was sweet, her markings and color emulating Sabre's, but she showed little interest in him while cuddling up to me. I told the breeder I didn't think that was going to work. Just as I was thinking about leaving, she said she had another one we might like to meet. Her son brought the new candidate around to us.

She explained, "This puppy scored low in prey drive and protectiveness. She's very submissive and the other German Shepherds pick on her. So, we have to keep her with the Border Collies."

I watched as Sabre stood back, allowing her to approach. She stopped and studied Saber, but showed no fear. He didn't move. She tentatively edged closer until she was standing in front of him. He leaned over, softly nuzzling her face.

Instantly, they took off into the taller grass, running and chasing each other like school kids turned out of class early. Sabre stopped, stretched his paws out in front and lowered his head, with his rear perched high in the air. Nissa ran in circles around him. Heather and I watched as they played until, exhausted, she plopped down on the ground to rest. Sabre stood behind her, refusing to lie down, keeping his attention fixed on me, as if to tell me, "This is the one I want." He displayed no confusion in his intent.

Chuckling, I walked over to the truck for my checkbook. Sabre and I decided her name would be Nissa, which translated from German, means a happy little girl.

When we started to leave, Nissa boisterously leaped into the back, then nestled into the space on the floor behind the seat as if nothing could be more natural. Sabre made several attempts to jump in behind her, each time dropping back to the ground as if he couldn't figure out how to get in. I patted the area of the seat that he could easily reach, but still he resisted. He moved back and forth between the back door and the front. He wanted a puppy, but that didn't mean he wanted her to ride in his back seat! Somehow I convinced him he didn't have a choice, but he stood on the seat, refusing to lie down as we started our trip back home. Riding with the back to himself was his domain. He could find no reason to give up the unrestricted view through either window, or the open floor where he turned around. He had no intention of sharing. If I wouldn't make Nissa move, he'd simply crawl over the console to join me in the front.

Sabre's efforts to get away from this intruder were laughable, but each time I blocked his attempts to escape. Finally, in resignation, he sat with his haunches on the back seat, his front legs on the floor, and lowered his head onto the console to avoid having to look at her.

Occasionally, he renewed his efforts with an almost panicked look on his face that said, "She doesn't belong here; this is my back seat! You never told me she was going to ride with me!"

Once we returned home, his discomfort was forgotten. He stayed by her side as Nissa explored the house, stopping when she hesitated, gently urging her to continue through reassuring nudges with his nose. He stood back as she sampled the water in his bowl and dedicated his full attention to encouraging her comfort in her new surroundings.

As they settled in together, I was fascinated by what seemed to be Sabre's dedicated mission to insure Nissa's welcome and build her confidence. He invented a game I dubbed "mouth to mouth combat." They lay on the floor, pretending to fight with their mouths wide open and their teeth gnashing, Nissa's head often completely within his powerful jaws. The sounds of their escalating growls filled the room. The game invariably ended with kisses, grooming, and an occasional nap.

Sabre's approach seemed choreographed, wearing down her timidness, strengthening her resolution, instilling in her the courage she hadn't been able to build. At the first sign that she was becoming frustrated, he would back off, allow her to win, and then make the game just a little bit harder the next time. His gentle, loving manner was touching. Despite my earlier hesitation, Sabre had shown me there was ample room in my heart for Nissa. Sabre had resolved both this timid little girl's lack of confidence and my doubts about becoming attached to another because of him.

Chapter 12
The Bunny Hop

One afternoon, I happened to glance down at the floor, where Sabre and Nissa were nestled so close to each other that they looked like a two-headed, two-tailed German Shepherd. I couldn't distinguish where one ended and the other began. I laughed out loud, rudely disturbing their quiet nap. This mingling of glossy dog fur became a commonplace floor decoration, two German Shepherds, as close as the air around them, content and happy.

I was finishing a design when Sabre and Nissa jumped up, running to the back door whining, barking, and growling. I looked through the glass of the door, but saw nothing out of place so I went back to work. They refused to settle down. Their persistent whining took on a desperate tone.

Since the occasional opossum travels along the top of the fence in search of food or while returning to a nearby den from a night of adventure and romance, I decided to investigate. My fierce hunters were delighted. Nissa immediately turned to her left, and abruptly stopped, staring up at the wooden highway. I was surprised that she didn't run to the fence and jump up in her usual ferocious manner. She stood without moving. Sabre not only stopped, he sat down, eyes glued to the puzzling, yet arresting sight.

A brown furry animal was perched on the edge, placidly looking down at us. The astounding creature hopped a few inches closer for a better look. No nervousness or worry was apparent, only interest from a vantage point of relative safety. I was astonished. I could not imagine how a rabbit could have gotten on top of the fence, much less navigated as far as my office door, but there was no mistaking the reality of the character that balanced on the thin ribbon of wood.

A staring match had begun, but even more perplexing than the fact that the rabbit had gotten there was the fact that neither dog was doing anything. Nissa would normally have thrown herself against the fence in an attempt to knock an opossum to the ground. Sabre would have stood at the base of the fence, using his powerful back legs to jump toward the top, trying to snag a foot or a tail. This time, they did nothing; they sat and stared. I moved a little closer, but the incredible rabbit didn't move at all. Head tilted to the side, eyes fixed on me, the prowler regarded us as we gaped at him. My eyes grew wide as I realized that I was seeing a squirrel without a tail. The graying muzzle and piercing eyes gave testament to myriad trials of living with a strength to be envied. A smile crept across my face, as my admiration for this grizzled survivor grew. His interest, however, apparently lagged and he started hopping toward the front yard. I told both dogs to come inside and they followed without hesitation in apparent homage to this worthy anomaly.

A few minutes later, when I walked into the kitchen for more coffee, I glanced toward the front windows. The Bunny Hop Squirrel had moved to the tree outside the breakfast nook and was quietly taking in the sights of his new people zoo. My fascination lingered. I stood at the window as he climbed higher in the tree, then jumped to the roof to continue his journey. I mimicked a respectful salute in admiration as he went on his way. Maybe the squirrels got the last word after all.

Chapter 13

Tasmanian Devil

In those first few weeks, I was learning that my sweet little Nissa, "Peanut" as I sometimes called her, was a Tasmanian devil disguised as a German Shepherd. She was full of energy, and Sabre had done his job of building her confidence far too well. In her exuberance to show a passing dog or cat that had wandered too close to her abode her bravery and aplomb, she barked at a level that I'm certain exceeded the recommended decibel limits for the human ear. To punctuate her budding aggressiveness, she leapt in the air, often snagging the blinds or striking the windows.

Sabre, by contrast, kept both feet on the floor. He knew he wasn't supposed to get on the furniture and apparently assumed the window sills were also off limits. The only exception was the necessary task of saving Milk-Bones behind the pillows on my bed. While he often placed his stuffed charges between the couch cushions and occasionally sniffed at objects on a low table, his sense of appropriateness was well-defined, his manners impeccable.

Not so Nissa; she was incorrigible. When I was around, she put on her "little angel" face, behaving nicely. The minute I left the house, the devil in her came out. She camped out on my bedspread, knocking pillows around with no effort to correct the disarray, and at night after every one had gone to sleep, she took over the couch. She ate CDs, leaving only slivers of plastic behind. She once read a paperback, leaving the ragged remnants in several rooms. Stuffed objects within her reach became the victims of murder most foul, puffs of white scattered indiscriminately wherever she dropped them with no effort to hide her deeds. In frustration one day, I pointedly asked Sabre why he didn't do something. That moment was the only time he refused to look me in the eye. In fact, he pointedly looked away. I turned toward the mess. I saw Sabre glance over at Nissa with a look that resembled amusement. I concluded they had a pact between them. Sabre's treasured charges were never touched or torn apart. My pillows, however, could not claim the same protection. Before she decided to grow up, I had replaced three window panes and two sets of blinds.

Each time I had a talk with her, she put on her sweetest you-can't-help-but-love-me face and pretended to agree, enthusiastically reverting to her wild-beast-in-the-wilderness ways as soon as I walked out the door.

One day, I growled at her in desperation, having exhausted all persuasive speech. A look of shock blanketed her eyes as she pulled her head up and back from my encroaching face.

"I've had it!" I told her emphatically.

That time, unlike our previous talks, I could sense that we connected, and something in her eyes seemed to change. If I had to guess, I would say that for the first time in our battles, she took me seriously. Maybe I should have resorted to growling before.

Sabre abandoned his position a safe distance away, coming up to Nissa, nuzzling her jaw with his muzzle, and then moving to my side. I sensed, too, that the pact had ended. The time had come for Nissa to grow up. I suspected that Sabre agreed.

The evidence of her resolve became her new routine. I no longer returned home to the destruction of a Texas tornado on a regular basis. She treated the house with respect and exercised restraint when I was gone. Sometimes, however, there were infrequent occasions when she reverted to old behaviors. I found nose prints on the windows from driving away wandering cats, and I discovered an impression on the couch with reddish dog fur on the fabric. With just a word, I'd let her know that I was aware of her indiscretions. The rules of the house were established, and peaceful coexistence was restored.

Chapter 14
The Great Pancake Debacle

Nothing about Texas weather competes with its summer. I often joked that the state only had three days of winter. The summers last forever. They are hot, humid, and conjure up excruciating visions of Hades. The normal pace slows to a creeping crawl, in keeping with the oppressive heat. Time spent outside, for Sabre and Nissa, lessened as they were drawn back inside to the comfort of the air conditioning. If left a minute too long outside, Sabre sat at the door, a beseeching look in his eyes, and Nissa slammed her paw against the window as if asking, "Hurry up, will ya?"

Summer also seems to have a particular sense of humor by marking the beginning of German Shepherd snow flurries. They start to shed their thick undercoats that once protected their ancestors from the elements when they ran wild through the open countryside. Their hair loosens in large, pointed tufts, protruding from their bodies, giving them the appearance of giant, multicolored porcupines. Their undercoats are as soft as rabbit fur or goose down. Even their legs have tiny white bumps of white dotting the surface.

While humans dread the season, dogs are not totally displeased, because they know they will be brushed more often. For my two, summer meant extra trips to the groomer. Nissa would prance out the salon door, showing off a pretty bandana that I'm sure she thought accentuated her wardrobe. Sabre knew without doubt that he was dashing, freshly bathed and brushed, and similarly adorned. They wore their new accessories for days after, until the ends began to unravel and I had to take them off. There was no great price to pay for their date with the groomer and a far better choice than an unceremonious bath with the hose in the back yard.

The middle of summer brings Fourth of July fireworks. The house in East Dallas was fortuitously situated for the greatest advantage. A few blocks to the northeast is the historic Dallas Country Club. A mile or two to the southwest is Fair Park, home of the State Fair of Texas and Big Tex. Directly west is downtown with the Trinity River Project. All three send an enormous amount of firepower skyward when the evening rolls in on the jubilant holiday. Neighbors gather in their front yards, in the street, or the little park across the way to watch the pyrotechnic display with the resounding booms that echo through the night air. To me, the best part was not having to look for a place to park.

Each year, Sabre enjoyed the show, mingling with his friends in the neighborhood, demonstrating, to their surprise, his lack of fear of the loud noises. I smiled at their remarks, knowing that to him, the fireworks were just another kind of lightning. Nissa thrived on the fact that they were the only two dogs not cowering under the bed, and that meant more attention for her. The added benefit for me was that Sabre didn't expect me to furnish air conditioning.

With the exception of those festivities, entertainment in this hellish season is limited to a short list of activities that can be enjoyed inside only. Since firing up a grill meant adding to the already impenetrable heat, I didn't own one. Instead, we enjoyed the opportunity to invite people over for a visit and offered a chance for me to try out emerging skills in the kitchen. I enjoyed the more gourmet aspects of dining, therefore, a meat and potatoes dinner held little appeal. Yet, without culinary talent, my challenge was to cook something I would also enjoy eating.

I started experimenting, using what little I knew and branching out in an effort to emulate my favorite restaurants. Sabre positioned himself where he could supervise or help in case of emergency, no matter that I spent half the time stepping over him. Nissa edged as close as she could to the action, in hopes that a tasty morsel might drop within her reach.

Steaks were easy, and my first attempts at Lyonnaise potatoes didn't turn out too bad. I discovered I could take plain mayonnaise, squeeze in lemon juice, and stir to create a passable sauce for a giant lump crab meat appetizer. I was also certain that I had observed enough times as bananas flambé was prepared at my table to be able to knock out the dish with no problem. My rather scanty supply of liquor didn't include Rum 151, so I settled for bananas Foster. Apparently, I missed one very crucial ingredient: rum in the butter and brown sugar sauce. When I poured the steaming mixture over ice cream, the sauce became the Big Rock Candy Mountain. No one could have eaten the mess without a hammer and chisel to break it up first. If I'd had the poor judgment to offer the sauce to the dogs, they would have had be fitted with dentures afterward. Later efforts were tastier and not as hard on the teeth when I figured out what was missing. I considered saving a portion to chunk at impertinent squirrels.

I thought Sabre was a little disappointed that I created few failures to end up as flavoring for his dog food. As I cleaned up the kitchen, Nissa left with a snort of derision because I had also failed to drop any food on the floor. I told her that maybe in her next life she'd get a human who was a klutz, and I chuckled to myself.

One weekend, I fully redeemed myself in the eyes and stomachs of my two companions. I'd remembered a couple of years ago when I watched Lynda, a fellow camping enthusiast, whip up a hearty breakfast of pancakes and bacon in the hill country of Texas. She had mixed the batter in a bowl and poured circles of white paste in a skillet. I watched the bubbles dance on the surface as she flipped them over to brown on the other side. I thought to myself, *How hard can that be? After all, I'd mastered Bananas Foster.* On Saturday morning, I decided to try. Having purchased the mix, I put the box on the counter, read the directions, and gathered the ingredients. While I religiously followed the directions, my mouth started to water thinking about breakfast at my front windows, a good book to read, and a great way to kick off the next two days.

My batter looked like hers and smelled sweet like hers, so I poured some into the skillet. I watched contently as the bubbles rose to the top and burst. I breathed in the fragrance of the warming concoction, while running through the list of possible toppings in my mind. I silently congratulated myself for my certain success. Both dogs sat as close as they could to the action, alert with all four ears perked forward, eyes following my every move. They watched me as I watched the batter, when the thought popped up, unbidden, that I didn't know when to flip them over. Lynda had made the process appear easy, even graceful, carrying on conversations with people at the same time. Asking Sabre or Nissa would have done no good. I wisely deduced that there was no time to call anyone on the phone for help. Fortunately I thought to lift up the edge with a spatula to see if it was brown. Panic avoided, I relaxed.

While I was distracted with these technical issues of the culinary arts, I failed to notice that the small circle of batter I'd initially placed in the pan was getting larger. The tiny amount had now expanded to twice the original size, and showed no signs of slowing. I checked quickly to see if the bottom had gotten brown. There was no indication, but the pancakes were still growing. The incredible mass had expanded to two thirds of the size of the skillet, continuing to get larger. There was still no hint of brown on the bottom. The bubbling blob edged over the sides and began to flow over the top I tossed the spatula aside and thought about running to the truck for a shovel. By that time, both dogs were leaning toward the stove. I don't know if dogs can grin, but if not, they gave a close approximation. In the second or two that I turned to look at them, the anticipated pancake breakfast became an entity from a horror movie and cascaded to the floor. The monster was eating my stove! Sabre and Nissa danced with anticipation. I grabbed the skillet and threw it into the sink. I turned the water on, and then looked back over at the ruined stove.

Both of my canine companions were joyfully licking up the mess from the stove and the floor, rotating from stove to floor and back again, darting around each other in canine ecstasy. What else could I do? I laughed.

After I finished cleaning up the mess, I tossed the spatula and the blue skillet that had now turned white into the dishwasher. I ushered my zealous rescuers to the back yard. In my most official voice, I informed them both that if they were so anxious to help with housecleaning, I'd spray Pledge on their tails and they could dust when they came back in. They weren't impressed. I guessed I should have been grateful that the alien pancake blob didn't try to eat the refrigerator, too.

The Great Pancake Debacle over and forgotten, I moved on to fish and other savory items, enjoying the process and the company my cooking afforded. Sunday afternoons provided opportunities for highlighting my latest efforts. Our most frequent guests were Marty and Gloria, and their two grown up puppies, Holly, and Candy. Although I questioned any laudable degree of success where cooking is concerned, they assured me the food was good, nobody got sick and had to go to the hospital, and they were willing to come back. I concluded that my cooking wasn't a failure, and the gatherings were fun.

Candy decided she didn't like Nissa living with her self-appointed beau and became grumpy whenever Nissa neared. Nissa reverted to her lifelong frantic submissiveness, desperately trying to win Candy's approval amidst the growls and snapping teeth at our social events. Sabre watched but rarely moved in between them. He figured the humans were doing an adequate job.

Candy was jealous of the impudent little upstart and no amount of cajoling or correction could persuade her otherwise. Holly, however, delighted in Nissa's company, running and playing and cavorting in the back yard, enjoying a comfortable camaraderie in the house. Candy forever remained convinced that Sabre was her Valentine and nothing would change that fact.

Chapter 15
Sole Survivor

Having gained Nissa, Holly, and Candy for his pack, Sabre decided to add a few humans, as well, and he had a very special initiation for each. When an unsuspecting visitor passed his requirements, his first objective was making certain that they were free of fleas.

First, he administered his standard sniff test. Then, allowing them ample time to show their adoration, he started to "flea" them the same way dogs do among their own, rapidly working his teeth up and down against their skin. This pinching maneuver was designed to catch unwanted vermin and crush them. The only problem in doing the same thing with humans was that they didn't have a thick layer of fur protecting their tender skin.

Sabre didn't mind if they yelped a little bit; he was granting a very special gift. As his startled inductees rubbed their stomachs, he stood back wagging his tail with obvious pride. Maybe he thought, *What's a couple of bruises among friends?*

The graciousness of my two pooches also encompassed one of the wild cats that roamed the neighborhood. Nissa played her role in helping choose the recipient of this honor. Primarily because of Sabre's patient mentoring, Nissa had gained a proprietary view of her premises and the courage to back up her opinion from behind the perceived safety of the windows. She had learned the boundaries of home from the sidewalk to the front door from her walks. When squirrels and cats invaded her undisputed turf, they were treated to ferocious growling and barking.

Calico Cat escaped her customary threats, the singular exception to their "no cats allowed" rule. Whenever she wandered over, both dogs stood at the window, making no aggressive moves. Calico stared through the windows at them before stretching out in the grass for an afternoon nap. Sabre stood quietly beside Nissa, tail slowly wagging, contemplating this graceful, fearless feline. The communication between them established a zone of comfort among natural combatants. That courtesy seemed to also extend to me. If I walked out to get the mail, Calico Cat paid slight notice, her eyes taking in my movements. She displayed no tenseness or fear, despite her reputation for never getting too close. She remained in her place, swishing her tail slowly back and forth.

I was alarmed one afternoon when I entered the kitchen to see both dogs sitting at the front windows observing the view outside. Ears pitched forward, neither moved, no tails wagged, and they barely seemed to breathe. Out in the yard, Calico Cat was sprawled on her back in the grass, paws in the air, tail stretched out behind, with not a hair mussed on her body. I was overwhelmed with a sense of sadness, thinking she was dead, but perplexed that neither dog seemed overly concerned. I studied her for a moment, finally noting the subtle rising and falling of her chest in the regular rhythm of dreams. Calico Cat was comfortably snoozing with her two sentinels standing by to warn of impending danger.

We had another scare a few nights after. I was startled out of the warm, cozy veil of sleep by the sounds of Sabre and Nissa tearing through my bedroom at 2:30 in the morning, furiously barking, heading straight for the window closest to the backyard. Somewhere beneath the canine clamor, I could hear the thump and rattle of the gate. I turned on the floodlights to see the gate bulge out from the bottom and vibrate back into place, only to swell out again and again from the noisy bombardment. Someone had crept into the backyard and was kicking at the gate in a futile attempt to escape. I cracked open the window and yelled at the intruder, "If you're not gone in thirty seconds, I'm letting these dogs out after you."

I had to laugh later at the thought of turning the dogs loose. The last thing I would do is expose them to danger especially considering that I had a .357 magnum not more than eight feet from my grasp. Of course, in Texas, everyone has two or three guns, at least. My ruse worked. The noise stopped, and when the police arrived a couple of minutes after I called them, there was no sign of the errant visitor.

Sabre and Nissa weren't willing to abandon their moment of glory and proceeded to inform the two officers of their prowess and determination. Their pride was conspicuous in having successfully chased the danger away. Because of their accomplishment, they both seemed to agree, they were justifiably deserving of a treat. As I walked back through the door, they headed for the kitchen and then to the cabinet where I kept their rewards for outstanding guardianship.

Over the years, I'd derived a few conclusions about dogs as compared to people. I didn't have thousands of dollars of research results from laboratory studies, only years of living day to day with my German Shepherds. Dogs exhibit the same emotions as humans. There are definite and identifiable changes in their behavior that indicate happiness, such an excited bark, a wagging tail, and the brightness in their eyes when given attention from the person they love.

They show sadness when their shoulders sag, or their ears fall toward the floor in a forlorn look that blunts all other expressions. They show anger, an older dog becoming antagonistic when a pesky puppy, having been chased away, returns to pester and annoy. Fear is obvious when a resounding clap of thunder rattles the sky and the earth below trembles in response. Frustration, anxiety, uncertainty, all the feelings associated with stress has a physical impact in their eyes, their breathing, and if one were close enough listen, in their heartbeats, as well.

They lack the cold manipulations that people assign to each other when their greed reigns over any concern for fairness or consequence. They are not motivated by guile, although a dog will identify or seek advantage. This instinct is imprinted in the timeless need for survival. They have no ego to satisfy and are free to love without reservation, to the point of self sacrifice if called upon by circumstance.

Their communications can outdistance the reliance that human beings place on words, perhaps, with greater value for the purity and honesty. A dog will not hurt someone close to them just to watch a pain-filled grimace fall across someone's face for the satisfaction of payback for a perceived wrong.

I doubt there has ever been a single dog owner that has not said, "If only they could talk." They do talk. Their language is explicit in their entire being. I also suspect they are not lacking, in a sense of humor. Neither Sabre nor Nissa ever revealed the secret of Calico Cat's uniqueness. I guess I wasn't on their "need to know" list.

One afternoon, I was answering an e-mail from a particularly demanding client, one of those people who refused to be happy even when their requests were fully accomplished. Sabre sat by my chair, in his usual quiet manner, waiting for me to notice him. When I finally looked up, he had closed his mouth, but his upper lip was trapped over his tooth, according him a goofy expression. If he could have married thoughts to words, he'd have asked me, "Is it really that important?"

I started laughing. Nissa came bounding in and all three of us ended up cavorting on the floor. I reached up, hit the send key, and we went out back to play.

Not only was Sabre sensitive to my moods, he was also attuned to events I couldn't begin to explain. His awareness encompassed phenomena far exceeding the limits of my mind. Since thunderstorms were on his most favored entertainment, I was perplexed when he insisted on waking me early one morning during a particularly vigorous autumn storm. Thunder threatened to rip apart the sky and lightening charged the air. I first thought his urgency was a need to go outside, so I headed to the back to let him out. Instead of bounding into the yard, he stood back, whimpered, and looked up at me, as he edged back from the door. He turned toward the kitchen and the front window closest to my neighbor's house. He stared through the glass, and then again looked up at me. The intense illumination from the storm failed to show anything amiss, but I'd learned to trust him. I got a flashlight from the office, as Nissa followed a few steps behind. I pointed the beam between the houses, and all I could see was a river of water rapidly flowing along the adjacent dwelling. His whining grew more desperate, and I opened the window to counter the reflection of the flashlight.

Finally, I located the object that had seized his attention. At the juncture of the fence at my neighbor's house, one of the neighborhood cats had stashed a litter of kittens against the foundation and they were engulfed in water. The mother was staring down at them, not knowing what to do. I bolted out into the deluge, paying no attention to the icy pelting rain. The closer I got, the louder the mother cat growled. Along with the crashing storm, her raw animal sounds were a sorrowful torture, a combination of fear and hopelessness, corresponding to Sabre's distress and urgency.

A quick glance told me that the mother was young and the litter was likely her first. No other conclusion was possible from the site she had chosen for her nest. She backed away as I approached. Of the four litter mates, three were already dead, but when I picked up the fourth, I heard a weak, pitiful mewl. Grabbing this last survivor up, I ran back into the house where Sabre met me at the door, matching my steps. I wrapped the tiny creature in a towel. Holding the newborn close to my chest, I grabbed a microwave hand warmer and set the timer. I tested the temperature first, and then wrapped the pad in the towel to warm the struggling kitten. I used my finger to clear its mouth and airway to stop the pitiful coughing. Massaging the undeveloped muscles and feeling the ribs poking out from the skin, I uttered a silent prayer that this life would be saved.

I waited for signs of agitation to subside, watching as the fledgling settled into the surrounding warmth. Sabre nudged my arm; he wanted to see. I watched with tears streaking down my cheeks, as he tenderly licked the kitten's face and then sat back, apparently satisfied. The time, in red numbers on the stove, foretold the impossibility of sleep for the remaining hours of the morning. With the kitten clutched close in one arm, I put on a pot of coffee, and the two dogs and I withdrew to the living room.

We passed the hours reheating the microwave pad, dripping a mix of honey and water on the kitten's tongue, and hoping to provide a little strength. I fervently hoped for its survival. As with his tail and ears before, Sabre seemed to think I could fix anything. This time, I wasn't so sure.

Eventually the storm passed with only the remnants of its fury visible in the brief faded flashes of far away lightning. Outside, I could hear the miserable keening of the mother, mourning her lost brood, and searching for the kitten I'd taken from her. I longed for a language she could understand to tell her that I was keeping her baby warm.

When morning arrived, I loaded up the dogs, and I placed the kitten in a box with the towel and a freshly warmed pad. I remembered a vet's office close by. They gave directions to a rescue facility. Sabre and Nissa rode quietly.

A helper at the second office took the box from my arms. "Does it have a name?"

"Soul Survivor," I said without thinking. I watched her carry the box through the door.

The mother hung around the house for several days afterward, her desolate cries piercing the quiet with an unrest that permeated the air. Although I didn't hear her for a while, she still came back day after day, unwilling to give up the quest for her lost brood. Sabre went to the window and stood each time he heard her, and Nissa lay down at his feet with her head on the window sill. They silently acknowledged the sounds of grief.

I learned, several days later, that Soul Survivor had survived and was adopted by a family whose cat had been lost in the same storm. They kept the name I had given.

Chapter 16

Famous, By Proxy

From the first day this adult puppy came to live with me, people stopped to admire Sabre, pleased when he welcomed their attention. I told them that Sabre was "famous, by proxy." Their quizzical looks always brought a smile or a laugh, as I explained that his brother, Tico, was the 2005 German Shepherd Dog Club of America Herding Victor. His sister Shay had earned the title of champion and other awards of accomplishment, and brother Tex held multiple titles for high scoring in obedience. I figured that made Sabre almost royalty.

The teamwork of Letty and her partner, Kathleen, spanning decades of hard work through Chaos Kennels had, indeed, turned chaos into beauty with a litter of stars. Their dedicated research and devotion to the German Shepherd breed had paid off with outstanding results. Motivation was summed up by a single sentence on their website: "The goal was a beautiful, competitive conformation dog with the will and the intelligence to work and compete in performance competition and the patience to be a good household companion."

I've been fortunate in getting to know breeders whose integrity embraced a sincere desire to preserve and enhance the breed. First was EJ, who researched and studied for months before deciding on a particular breeding, and who produced champions too numerous to count. She claimed many champions that also produced champions, obedience winners, and dogs who took their places in innumerable homes as treasured family members.

Breeders, however, seem to be either lauded or cursed in these present days. I believe in the mission of rescue groups and join wholeheartedly in the rant against breeders who are only interested in financial gain or status. But, preservation of distinct breeds is a valid goal. I couldn't imagine a world without this noble and regal breed, or the other breeds also distinctive for their attributes. Letty and Kathleen fall into the category of the breeders I've chosen to associate with over the years, the ones who care more for the breed than producing puppies for money. The costs involved in a producing a single litter is not insignificant and would be appallingly foolish to a financial adviser.

I remembered EJ once telling me that a German Shepherd is bred to be either totally at work or totally at rest. This trait was apparent in every one I've owned for over forty years, along with their abilities to learn, to faithfully perform the tasks expected of them, and to love with every part of their being. Mine have all been affectionate and adoring, always ready to go, and just as happy to get back home. While the general belief is that a grown German Shepherd has the intellectual equivalent of a fourteen-year-old human, I probably would have agreed before Sabre. My perception was that he was much wiser than me in countless ways, sometimes redefining ideals I'd held for years.

Males and females seem to differ in their requirements for affection. Females seem more independent; they want attention when they want attention; otherwise, they can't be bothered. When German Shepherd males are feeling cuddly, normally twenty-four hours of each day, they give a new definition to the phrase "puppy love." Sabre was no exception. Second only to being brushed on his list of favorite activities was having his belly rubbed. I often knelt on the floor beside him, slowly stroking his stomach and sometimes scratching behind his ears at the same time. Laughter was inescapable as he rolled his eyes and emitted ecstatic snorts that resembled thunder, starting loud, reverberating along the cool travertine floor, and finally abating in small contented bursts of air.

By comparison, Nissa seemed embarrassed by his terribly undignified behavior. She flopped onto the carpet with a groan, refusing to look in our direction. My happy little girl had her own design for the proper belly rub. Hearing the announcement for bedtime, she ran to the bedroom. She seized her place at the side of the bed, and then flipped over on her back, steadying herself with one paw firmly planted against the mattress. Head lolling off to the side and all four feet in the air was her official declaration that time had come for a Nissa Special belly rub. If I didn't respond fast enough, she'd raise her head to stare at me, until I slipped off my house shoe, and stroked her stomach with my foot. I laughed at the sight of an upside down dog, tail blissfully sweeping left and right. She made her intent quite clear that the time to quit was her decision, not mine.

Sometimes on a leisurely week end morning, I looked down to see them crowding my chair so closely that I couldn't change position without running a wheel over one or the other. I calculated that the three of us occupied approximately nine square feet of space, and I wondered why I was paying for the rest of the house. They were content lying at my side, napping with one eye half open, but ready for anything that might come their way.

Sabre was no longer "too much trouble." He loved his home, his human, and the puppy he had chosen. Nissa had her protector and playmate. I had my dream dog and my sweet "baby girl." Watching them together became almost a hobby, second only to selecting the next stuffed toy to join Sabre's menagerie.

Chapter 17

Henrietta, the Perennially Suffering Fowl

Trips to the store to buy dog food inevitably included grabbing up chew sticks for Nissa and a perusal of all the toys to find one that Sabre would like. One such errand included the discovery of Henrietta, the perennially suffering rubber fowl. Second only to the gorilla that laughed maniacally, was this tall, skinny parody of a chicken wearing a Santa Hat, a skimpy red skirt that flared out at the bottom, and black motorcycle boots.

When squeezed, Henrietta screamed in agony, and Sabre immediately bolted to her rescue. Grabbing up this loudly disruptive, tormented creature, he would search the house diligently for a place where Henrietta could gain relief, causing me to howl with laughter. The more I laughed, the more he searched. He removed her to another location where he obviously decided she would be safer. I couldn't resist walking by and poking her with my foot to make her scream again so I could watch his almost frantic efforts to deliver Henrietta's wretched soul from torment. Then, I'd look over at Nissa, her commentary causing even more merriment. One eye cocked above the other, ears pointing in different directions, and a disgusted groan, her expression proclaimed her apparent assessment, "What's all the fuss? It's just a toy!" The game always ended with getting out his brush, grooming his lustrous coat, and Nissa prancing off to her front windows.

Sabre could not tolerate distress among those he considered in his charge. He had found that his ultimate job was to comfort and console. Once deprived of attention and affection, he had transformed his longing into a gift of compassion.

Of all the toys I'd bought him, one was his obvious favorite. Hedgehog became the ultimate German Shepherd puppy for

Sabre and the plaything that drew the most attention. A stranger coming into the house caused Sabre to grab Hedgehog and look for the most secluded corner he could find. When Nissa plopped down close, she signaled that his giant stuffed toy needed to be moved. Few people earned the honor of having Sabre share his treasured possession with them.

This ungainly imitation was larger than the other toys. Although Henrietta claimed the distinction of being tall, she was skinny. Gorilla was wider but short, and Jake the duck was long and compact. Hedgehog was the size of a six or seven-week-old pup and had all the right colors to be part of the clan. I often went into the kitchen to see Sabre lying comfortably at the windows, Hedgehog between his paws. I had to stop him daily from carrying his favored companion outside to keep the dirt and leaves from sticking to it. There was no doubt that this was his king of toys. Hedgehog alone brought out a protectiveness that was unmatched.

Chapter 18

Dumped

Neither dog liked being left at home while the other got to ride in the truck, although they were rarely asked to put up with such inconvenience. They went to the groomer together; they went for visits together; even a short jaunt to the store meant that both would share the trip. By then, Sabre had resolved his initial unwillingness to share his back seat. He and Nissa vied for the windows, stepping over and around, and if their maneuvering didn't produce the desired result, they sat on each other.

Sometimes, the occasion demanded that one be left behind. One such excursion was for a visit to Ronnie for shots. In the outer room, Sabre waited patiently for his turn, checking out the latest dog food and treats on the shelves, noting the smells of the floor and chairs, and charming all those around him. There, as well as other places we went, he was remembered. When possible, the staff came over to greet him. He seemed massive compared to the other dogs around him, but his gentle manner belayed their apprehension.

Moving to the examination room only provided new smells and diversions, while the glass door enabled him to keep track of who or what came and went as we waited. After saying hello to Ronnie, Sabre settled down in his private area, knowing Ronnie and I would chat for awhile before getting down to business. He seized the opportunity to sneak a look through the other door to the back area to see what everyone else was doing.

His turn soon came. He loved attention, and nothing could be better than being the star attraction plus getting to play the role of patient. No matter what the occasion, no matter what he was asked to do, or where he was, he found a reason to be happy and expressed his gratitude with generous kisses. Every dinner was justification to come to me with his special thanks; a ride in the truck was certain to produce a few kisses on the ear as I drove. On one of those visits, Ronnie's face edged into range and Sabre delivered a slurp worthy of a hand towel, and then sat back, wagging his metronome tail, quite satisfied with his accomplishment. His supply of kisses was unlimited.

A few months after that visit to the vet, an unusual and unprecedented event occurred. I'd taken Sabre with me on one of those rare errands by himself. Especially when the dogs were with me, an exceptionally heightened state of awareness was necessary, even demanded when behind the wheel. I concentrated on maintaining a wide space back from the car in front and keeping to streets where speed could be kept to a minimum. Drivers in Dallas weren't predisposed to caution in their driving habits; sometimes appearing as if they were actively trying to hit each other. Therefore, I exercised care in anticipating traffic lights, watching the side streets for drivers showing any signs of inattentiveness, and staying focused on pedestrians who might wander into our path.

For no reason that I could discern, the car in front of me hit the brakes and caused me to stop faster than normal. I wasn't going fast, maybe thirty or thirty-five miles per hour, but the halt was abrupt. Sabre ended up in the floorboard. Our momentum safely halted, I looked back to see if he was all right. The expression on his face was one I'd never seen before, and thankfully, never saw again after that incident. A look of accusation seemed to impart, "You did this to me!" I sensed that he was mad at me, holding me to blame for the fall.

I pulled into a parking space, apologizing profusely. Thankfully, as quickly as the look had appeared, his unspoken declaration vanished. We continued on our way, but I couldn't forget the feeling. Months would pass before I learned the significance.

Later that evening when bedtime approached, I turned the television on and stumbled onto a documentary featuring meerkats. The Animal Planet chronicles had become a popular series. I'm not an avid TV watcher. I prefer to read or occupy time with something more active. These intriguing creatures of diminutive size, lively mannerisms, and animated features captivated me with their daily struggle in the forbidding desert.

A young female in the group was fascinated, standing up on her haunches to stare at a hyena lurking around their perimeter. She stood on her back legs, tail stretched out for balance, mesmerized as the others prepared for sleep. During the night, however, she edged too close. When dawn painted the desert with the first rays of light, the others awoke to find her badly mauled. Despite their pressing need to find new shelter and new places to forage, they refused to leave her side until her spirit left her broken body. Their tenderness, the caring, and the devotion in that poignant story remained with me.

When I found the meerkat series on Animal Planet, I became a devoted fan. I followed their adventures, celebrated their pups, and memorized their names. I absorbed the excitement of their lives on the African desert. Watching the slithering snakes, stalking hyenas, birds of prey, and marauding bands from other meerkat families pursued the tribe on the screen, those predators became my enemies, as well. I often found myself pulling both feet onto the couch, fear growing when their adversaries came too close. I wanted to protect them. Sabre edged close, laying his head in my lap, as my emotions became embroiled in their struggles. I held onto him. His strong presence was invariably calming. He comforted and consoled me simply by being close. As dependent as he was on me for food and shelter and care, I had become just as dependent on him for my own sense of well-being. Sabre was my anchor; I knew he would never let me down.

Chapter 19
Platypus Cat Attack

While I grumped about the annoying sameness of all the chores that had to be done, and enjoyed the occasional surprise or diversion, some routines were oddly settling. All the upheavals and irritations of living dissipated through the walks with my pups around the neighborhood, bringing a sense of serenity at the end of the day. I took each dog for separate excursions. Neither particularly liked being left behind, but I discovered that taking them both resulted in tangled leashes and the very real possibility of one or both arms being dislocated at the shoulder. However, this was a dilemma of my own creation.

At the apartment, I never expected Sabre to heel or stay close. Touring the grounds was a chance for him to discover freedom. Nissa, of course, followed Sabre's lead, wildly pulling at the lead when anything caught her interest. The obvious solution was to take each for a walk individually. I'm sure we were quite the spectacle in an area where people could be seen any time of the day enjoying a stroll with their canine companions respectfully ambling along beside them. Tiny breeds, mutts, alluring golden retrievers, and labs were well-behaved and almost placid in their demeanor.

The wild behavior of my two free spirits was quite a contrast. They darted around chasing after squirrels, terrorizing the untamed cats with an abandon that appeared to border on incorrigible, yet "this way" brought each of them back to my side without urging or having to raise my voice. On the occasions I could let them run free of their leashes, they would return when called, abandoning the pursuit that had taken them too far away. What anyone else thought didn't bother me, because I could depend on Sabre and Nissa to respond immediately to whatever I asked of them. If they were happy, I was happy, and in an odd sort of way, I believed they were entitled to misbehave occasionally. They had earned that freedom by events in their past, but mainly through their reliable adherence to the few rules I had for them.

As with Sabre, remnants of Nissa's previous life were apparent, especially in the ways she responded to other dogs. My imagination engendered visions of her having to grovel at the feed bowl, bullied by her own kind, and probably not getting enough to eat. She had lived in fear of the dogs around her that had judged her weak. What Sabre had sensed in her, I also felt, not only a need to protect and nurture, but an appreciation of her sweetness and her ability to love without barriers.

One night shortly after she arrived to round out our trio, she screamed out in the night. I had never considered dogs having nightmares, but her apparent bad dream told a poignant story. Sabre and I had both rushed to her side to comfort her from the demons of sleep. I never forgot the heartrending sound of her cry. Only thirteen months old, slightly smaller than the norm for her age, she looked even younger and more fragile as she automatically rolled on her back in typical submissive posture at our approach. We stayed at her side for several moments, stroking her head and assuring her that everything was okay, that she was safe. When she calmed down, I brought her to the bedroom to sleep by my bed. As she settled into sleep, I vowed to erase her frightful memories. Sabre slept only a short distance away.

Nissa proved to be a fast learner, observing her protector barking fearlessly at his front windows to ward off impending danger. She rapidly adopted his guarding stances, ferocious barking, and added her own low growls and somewhat squeaky barks to the melee. Anyone daring to come onto the front porch was treated to a cacophony of threats and the sight of two determined German Shepherds only the width of a pane of glass away.

Sabre had also become the neighborhood expert at ferreting out cats that believed they were hidden from his sight. Regardless of the height of the grass, or the bush sought out for cover, they could not hide from his roving eye. I kept enough control of the leash to keep him from getting too close, more out of concern for him. I didn't want him to suffer a scratched nose, or worse, a well-connected claw to an eye. I didn't want the cats to get hurt, either. They seemed not to realize that they were easy prey, but the fact that they chose the same places day after day provided a reliable hint as to where they were likely to be found.

One pewter gray feline kept to a particular house. I dubbed him The Platypus Cat. Our less than quiet approaches caused him to flatten himself against the ground, ears back, chin dug into the earth, tail laid out behind, and his eyes as large as a yellow-tinged full moon rising. Sabre also played the game. He sniffed through the grass, gradually positioning himself closer before invading the last modicum of space. He then sprang into action. Platypus Cat rose on all four feet, arched his back, and fluffed his tail to double size, and hissed and spit. He growled his threats of serious bodily harm. After a few seconds of the best drama in the neighborhood, I pulled on Sabre's lead and we continued on our way. I'm sure Platypus Cat was certain he had imparted fear of great magnitude to that impertinent dog, while Sabre usually provided the finale with a rendition of his happy dance.

On her turn, Nissa followed in his footsteps, terrorizing the same cats Sabre had traumatized just moments before. She lunged at them, her barks revealing her delight more than any impending damage to their safety. They rewarded her with the same arching backs, hisses, and growls granted to the previous interloper.

Chapter 20

A Happy Little Girl

After cooling down from their respective walks, the time finally arrived for their favorite activity of the day. These expectant beneficiaries adopted their own routine for what to do while waiting for food. They lay on the floor close to the sink while I washed their bowls, watching as I mixed the ingredients in their dinnerware. Their eyes never left my hands as I added vitamins, then flavoring, and finally went over to the pantry for dog food. Both dogs followed in hopes that I would drop a few kibbles on the floor. I learned not to be too careful. They were happy.

Sabre then wagged his tail and stood beside his Charlie Brown mat. After placing his bowl on the floor, Nissa began a backward dance, front paws in the air, hopping backwards to her mat with her eyes glued to her dinner.

When Nissa first arrived, Sabre stood aside to allow her to eat with him. He didn't seem to mind sharing, and I couldn't help but smile as I watched him nurturing her. As she grew older, I finally persuaded her that both bowls were not intended for her.

At any time of the day, Nissa perceived a need for food beyond the level of sustenance, resulting in her scouring the carpet for traces of snacks left behind. She diligently cleaned both bowls after dinner until they shined like a Marine's brass. The word "dinner" brought her out of a dead sleep, bounding into the kitchen where she could supervise preparations. Although on most days, she was aware of dinnertime before I looked at the clock. She appeared beside me like a ghost, gently nudging my arm or bumping me with her nose, then running a few steps away, looking up as if to tell me, "Come on; it's time." A tap on the floor with my foot brought her running, nose down like a bloodhound hot on the trail, to look for any dropped morsels. I started calling her "Miss Piggy."

I remembered Nissa's first dinner in her new home. Apparently she'd been fed dry food, and when her nose hit the water infused mixture, she darted backward from her bowl, nose dripping water on the floor, a look of horror on her face as if she thought I was trying to poison her. Even Sabre looked over at her, but he was more polite. I laughed out loud, and then with profuse apology, showed her the dry food mixed in. Once she tasted the flavorful concoction, she enthusiastically devoured her supper.

Using water in their food came in handy later when Nissa got older and began to gain a little more weight than she should carry. I changed her dog food, adding a bit more water, less flavoring, and a reduced amount of the new recipe. The water made her feel as full when she ate, but as she lost weight, I cut back on the water. I felt a little guilty, as much as she loved food, but I didn't want her to become one of the growing numbers of overweight dogs. She didn't really seem to notice as long as dinner was served on time. She was content; she truly became the "happy little girl" that her name implied.

Chapter 21
Neighborhood Terrors

Nissa was discovering her talents and abilities, as well. I'd been told that Nissa, as a pup, had scored low in the areas of protection and prey drive. As I watched her grow, I determined that she possessed the traits, but simply hadn't had the opportunity to develop them. Her alertness and confidence reached a level comparable to any sound, intelligent German Shepherd. Fur standing at attention along her back, ears pointed forward, she guarded against the diabolical squirrels, invading cats, and anyone walking by the home she claimed as her own. Sabre seemed to view her antics with an air of pride, like a mother dog surveying a perfect litter. If language had been within his capacity, I'm sure he'd have told me, "I knew it all along. She just needed a chance."

Ever vigilant, Nissa positioned herself at the front windows, chin resting on the sill, eyes darting from side to side, awaiting anything foolish enough to invade her turf. Sometimes, she became so exuberant that the decibels of her barking exceeding the pain threshold of my ears, so I had to calm her down. Not to be thwarted, she dropped to a level of growling so threatening as to convince the uninitiated that certain death awaited the next wrong move. Long after the perceived danger had passed, she continued to growl in spurts, finally reverting to her watchful commitment. No matter the number of times she was told to hush, she had to have the last word.

A dog's hearing is far superior to that of human capacity, and Nissa proved her ability one night. With a sharp bark, she jumped from the side of the bed and ran to the front, Sabre close behind her. Immediately awake, I slipped my feet into my house shoes and followed. On the way, I heard the sound of smashing glass nearby. By then, both dogs were barking furiously at two men across the street who had broken a car window and were trying to pry open the door. Mainly because the front of the house was dark and the entry set back from view, I decided to step out onto the porch.

With the ferocious noise of barking and growling at my back, I yelled, "The police are on the way!"

Shocked at being discovered, the two thieves ran to their car to make their escape. I doubted that my threat of police on the way carried near the impact of their probable fear of the dogs being released. They jumped into their beat up compact car and sputtered away. We had thwarted their mischief.

Our combined actions were only slightly out of order, but Nissa barked, Sabre growled, and I called 911. When the squad car arrived moments later, I was able to give a reasonable description of the two bandits and their vehicle, but the two officers declined to interview Nissa and Sabre when I offered.

For the next few minutes as we attempted to reclaim what was left of a night's sleep, Nissa's pride was obvious. She pranced through the house and returned to the windows to growl. Sabre and I followed her reluctance to part with her moment of glory with amusement. Our happy little girl had grown up and was quite obviously pleased with her accomplishment.

Chapter 22
My Best Friend Has a Tail

How do you explain that your best friend has a tail, two pointed ears, four legs, and an icy cold nose? How do you not notice when this friend treats anything you do as okay? How do you describe something that you constantly feel from a being that shows interest in everything you do? What title do you assign to a companion that never fails to arrive at your side when your day doesn't go the way you planned, that would defend you with his life, doesn't expect you to be perfect, and settles for whatever you have left to give at the end of each day?

I should have been the glue that held the three of us together. After all, I was the human and the "leader of the pack." I'd felt that way with every dog, but with Sabre, our roles manifested in a way that resisted description through words. His was a gentle strength that people often aspire to but attain with so much difficulty. I wondered what enabled him to be happy for no particular reason, to show his gratefulness for any touch, acknowledgment, or his nightly dinner. On his face and in his eyes, his contentment showed without wavering

The crude, jagged edges of living seemed to find their way into our lives on a regular basis. Sabre became the guardian angel that I could touch. He helped to heal the inevitable cuts and bruises that were the norm in a world full of people that wanted more than their fair share, or took without giving in return. My canine companion had no conditions for what I should do, for who I should be; all he wanted was to be with me.

I count as friends those from whom pleasure and enjoyment came when they offered their best without demands. Their visits were consistently anticipated and never long enough.

Sabre, however, was more than a friend; he was an example to follow.

An adult while still a puppy, Sabre found a puppy-like joy in daily walks and teaching Nissa how to play. He taught her to put her fear aside, and he allowed her to feel safe. He taught me that each day holds the promise of enjoyment, whether a nudge on the arm, his quiet presence, or a shared look that said "love is a blessing with no guile, no disguises, and no contingencies."

Sabre had a similar impact on everyone he met. I was often aware that people stared at him with an undefined fascination in their expressions that seemed equal to being hypnotized. Had he been human, his special gift would have been called "charisma." Sabre, through his gentle manner, imparted serenity with a wisdom that seemed to transcend human experience.

With a sense of amusement, I jokingly referred to our house as the "Bat Cave." Our walls held a peaceful calm imbued with laughter. With large trees on all sides, light was always at a soft, low level within our house, and even the Texas sun was held at bay. The end of each day signaled rest that restored the energy needed to take on the next day. Each beginning of a new day was a celebration, punctuated by the rhythmic thump of Sabre's tail at my bedside as he joyfully assisted me in waking to greet the day, but more, I suspected, to greet him.

There is truth in the saying that "nothing lasts forever," and I had no illusions. At the same time, immersed in that comforting tranquility, I also had no thoughts or expectations that anything would drastically change in our future. No more than I would leave the house and plan to have an accident, could I imagine that anything could possibly rob us of our good fortune.

Chapter 23

I've Fallen and I Can't Get Up

All was not, however, as appearances might indicate. Something lurked beneath the surface, not readily seen and only revealed in brief, subtle glances that slipped behind a veil of illusion. My thinking masked the manifestations as ordinary circumstance.

I began noticing that Sabre stumbled, though only a random divergence from his usual robust and rhythmic pace as we traversed the concrete highways surrounding the area. East Dallas is an older neighborhood, some of the houses dating back to the 1920s. The roots of trees, grown to huge dimensions over the years beside the sidewalks, had caused the cement to heave in some places with numerous large cracks along the way. I had also tripped on the rough terrain, especially when distracted. Consequently, the rare times Sabre tripped didn't seem particularly significant. He recovered as fast as he faltered, and I attributed the infrequent episodes to the condition of the paths we navigated. He didn't seem bothered, and I dismissed my concern, as well.

Then, something happened that I couldn't ignore. We had taken a short trip one Sunday afternoon to visit friends who lived about an hour's drive away. In his usual carefree manner, he explored the grounds, sniffing and inspecting, with Nissa close on his trail. Together they cavorted in the tall grass, and I was reminded of his first encounter with Nissa.

After the afternoon of frolic, I loaded my two happy pups back into the truck for the journey home. I was listening to music and watching the drivers around me, with an occasional glance at the passing scenery. I happened to look back, surprised that Sabre was down on the floorboard with his rear paws up in the air next to his head. Expecting to see him get back on the seat, I looked forward again before glancing back. He hadn't moved from his position; Nissa stared down at him, and then looked up at me. I quickly found a place to pull over.

Sabre had become wedged between the seats, as if he'd fallen backwards and landed on his tail. I was perplexed because there had been neither sudden change in direction or speed nor any apparent reason for him to fall. I lifted him onto the seat, amid multiple kisses to my ears and my face. I checked him for injury, a seat belt that could have entangled him, anything to explain this strange event. There was nothing.

I kept a constant vigilance for the remainder of the trip. When we got home, I examined Sabre for anything I might have missed in the tight confines of the truck. I also decided a trip to see Ronnie was needed. The next day, Monday, was Ronnie's regular day off, so I made an appointment for Sabre on Tuesday. During the next day, I kept an eye on him, observing his movement, looking for any sign to explain what I'd seen. He had always been such a powerful dog, his rear end capable of pulling with a tremendous strength that had, on occasion, threatened my balance when he leaped forward on the leash. Even with numerous examinations, I could find no answer, but a nagging feeling in the pit of my stomach wouldn't go away.

Before leaving the next morning, I pulled out every object I could find in the garage to fill the void between the two back seats. I stuffed pillows on top to create a soft platform to prevent what had previously happened. I left just enough space by the door for him to be able to put his front legs on the floor then jump up on the seat.

There was nothing in his demeanor on the trip to the vet that seemed anything but normal. He stared out one window, and then switched to the other. He sat up and leaned on the seat, or reclined, peaking up over the bottom of the window to watch the scenery. At regular intervals, he leaned forward to sneak a kiss on my ear, enjoying the ride and relaying his gratitude. When we pulled into the parking area and stopped, he was excited to have arrived, jumping from the back of the truck, and running around to take in all the sights and smells.

In the waiting room, he was interested in all the other visitors, stretching to bestow a "Sabre kiss" on a particularly beguiling lady lab. He checked the shelves for any new treats on display, and then calmly settled at my feet to patiently await his turn. Sunday seemed nebulous, except for the gnawing feeling in my stomach.

In his customary manner, Ronnie listened to my description of the events on our excursion, his hands exploring Sabre's legs and back, seeking signs of discomfort or tenderness, and then looking closely at Sabre's back toenails. There was no indication of discomfort in my willing patient. All he exhibited was his enjoyment of the attention and affection.

Ronnie suggested that we take Sabre out back to watch him move. New sights and smells were consistently on Sabre's agenda; he delighted in peaking at parts of the clinic he'd not seen before. Once again, I was amazed at this dog's ability to absorb insignificant phenomena with delight, turning the mundane into a joyous celebration of discovery as he slowed our progression to poke his nose into ever nook and corner. Once outside, he ran from corner to corner of the enclosure, only stopping to leave his reminder to any dogs coming along behind him that he had been there first. Ronnie asked me to call him back, and then allow him to run free, focusing on his gait.

Silence enveloped the space around us, as Ronnie considered what he'd seen. As I watched him mentally checking off each observation and thought, the nagging at the pit of my stomach became a chilling sense of fear. This was my German Shepherd of a lifetime, the dog I'd dreamed of since childhood. Nothing could be allowed to hurt him. I'd promised he would grow old with me, with every indulgence I could provide. I'd vowed to protect him, to care for him, to keep his world happy and safe. I frowned, holding back tears that were beginning to well up in my eyes, as I waited for Ronnie's verdict.

I listened as he listed a number of possibilities. I realized as he spoke that I was trembling. He described symptoms I should look for and emphasized that examination was too early to determine exactly what could be happening. He asked me to bring Sabre back a few weeks later, or earlier if I saw anything else of concern, but advised that testing at that time might be premature.

Since my first experience with Ronnie and Sabre, then with Nissa, I'd grown to appreciate the thoroughness with which he approached each concern. However, I sensed at that moment that our lives were changing, although how or what couldn't yet be discerned. He prescribed vitamins that Sabre obviously accepted as candy.

I drove home deep in thought. Sabre seemed to sense the feelings of confusion that boiled up within me, leaning forward from his back seat to nuzzle my arm and lick my ear, as if trying to abate my apprehension. When we walked in the door at home, Nissa ignored me and ran up to Sabre, sniffing every part of him. Finally satisfied with what she found, she returned to her routine of guarding the house from her front windows. I sat down on the floor with Sabre, gazing at his face, stroking his head, and telling him how much I loved him. He kissed my face and poked his nose under my arm. The moment passed, and I got up from the floor, still unable to completely shake a lingering sense of uncertainty and muted sadness, but consciously controlling my thoughts. I remembered Ronnie's caution not to jump to conclusions.

Chapter 24
Animals in the Computer

The rhythms of living gradually prevailed and, while I remembered the list of what to look for, we continued to enjoy walks, rides, and ice cube crunching parties. For a couple of weeks, nothing caught my eye and I started to hope that all was meaningless circumstance that would prove to be a false alarm. I maintained my vigilance, and though still present, the unsettled feelings began to diminish.

The back yard remained the perfect place for a game of chase, or for Sabre to arch into the underside of the holly hedge along the fence to scratch his back whenever the notion struck him. We went to visit Candy and Holly, or they came to visit us. The menagerie of stuffed animals continued to be hidden when strangers came into the house and Hedgehog still held the place of honor.

I remembered Ronnie's caution to watch his back legs for signs of stumbling or of dragging. He advised me to examine his toenails for indications of wear along the top. I hadn't noticed any differences. Sabre seemed the same.

A new project involved the assembly of a collage of music and sound effects as a birthday present CD for a friend. Both dogs were napping just outside of the office, when I clicked on a sound effect clip of two cats fighting. Immediately, the rampant barking of my two protectors drowned out the sounds emitting from the computer. I almost jumped out of my chair, turning to see them charging through the door in full attack mode, the hair on their backs standing at attention, the whites of their gnashing teeth competing with the light in the room. I started laughing and laughed until my sides started to hurt. When the clip ended, they both scurried around the room looking in corners and out the windows, running through the living room, returning in search of the phantom cats that had dared to disturb their naps. I couldn't resist. I played the clip again and the avalanche of barking started anew. Then I played sounds of pigs squealing. They stood at my chair, heads tilting one way then the other, then back again. They were fascinated and befuddled all at the same time.

After the horse whinny, the lion growl, and the dog whine, they figured out that these animals were trapped in the computer. Both of my brave companions rested their chins on the desk top and stared at the speakers and me. They had caught on to my little joke. In unison, they walked back to the living room, abandoning me to my obvious bad taste. For me, playing the sounds had been the most fun I'd had in days and my laughter died away slowly in spite of their disdain.

The next sound brought my vanquished worry back to the front of my mind, like a stain that won't come out of a piece of clothing. As Sabre walked from the living room to the office, I heard the unmistakable click of toenails striking the metal track holding the glass doors. I got up and let the dogs out, standing by the office door until they came back in, listening as he crossed the threshold. Again, as Sabre entered, I heard each back foot striking as he walked through. The sounds repeated at the glass doors. I sat down on the floor and called him over to me, telling him to lie down. When I picked up his back foot, I saw the tops of his back nails starting to show signs of wear. I couldn't catch my breath, as my throat seized. Sabre raised his head from the floor, staring up at me, as the acid taste of fear rose up in my mouth. I tried to remain composed and logical. I had to think through what I was seeing.

"Don't jump to conclusions," Ronnie had warned. The words became my mantra.

Chapter 25
Tomorrow Isn't Promised

Don't jump to conclusions, I repeated over and over in my thoughts, not realizing that I was saying the words out loud. I closed my eyes, forcing air deep in my lungs, and then exhaled slowly until I was breathing normally again. I looked back to see Sabre watching me.

When we were shown into the exam room, his gaze seemed to settle on me as I gathered my thoughts for a litany of observations to give Ronnie what he needed to know.

"Sabre doesn't seem any different," I began. "He's happy. He gets excited when we go for walks. He plays with Nissa. He doesn't act like anything's hurting him. But, when he fell off the seat, he was literally trapped on the floorboard. He couldn't get himself up. I had to stop the truck and put him back on the seat." I felt my throat closing and I barely managed to add, "I'm seeing signs where his toenails are starting to wear."

"How's his appetite? Any problems with elimination? Any problems getting up or down?"

"His appetite's fine. I haven't seen anything else unusual."

A minute passed while Ronnie thought. Finally, he suggested, "Let's take him out back and watch him move around."

Sabre furtively turned his head in every direction and poked his nose into the shelves as we made our way to the back. I didn't have to say he was happy because his metronome tail was a blur as we reached the enclosure. He sniffed his way from corner to corner and along the fence.

Ronnie was quiet, intently focusing on Sabre, but my mind was whirling with the wild fury of a Texas tornado. Sabre was my perfect German Shepherd dog, my dream dog. He didn't deserve to have anything wrong with him. I wanted to cry. I wanted to scream, but I remained silent.

"He could have a tumor on his spine, or a disc problem," he said, shocking me back to the grim reality of the moment, "or a malfunction of his thyroid. At his age, he might be starting to develop arthritis." He paused, carefully considering what he would say next. "It could also be a neurological disease, Cauda Equana is a possibility, central nervous system disorders."

I drifted away from the conversation again. My mind was struggling like two dogs fighting in an alley. I realized I'd been holding my breath. Ronnie's words had begun to scrape away at any illusions I'd been holding in hope of a false alarm. Something was wrong and wasn't going to go away.

"Let's go back into the office," Ronnie finally softly suggested.

"Come on, Sabre!" I called.

He ran back to us and I clipped the lead into his collar. Sabre settled comfortably in front of the glass door, not wanting to miss the parade of people and animals checking in and out.

I'm gonna faint and fall on the floor, I thought. At that moment, I knew what being shot with a stun gun felt like, and I grappled with standing. My hands were firmly planted on the edges of the examination table, but my knuckles were white with tension.

I was grateful when Ronnie started running his hands over Sabre because I didn't have to try to talk. He carefully felt along Sabre's spine, probing deep into the spaces between the bones. He lifted Sabre's tail, moving up, then down, and side to side. Pulling first one back leg, then the other, he moved each through the full range of motion. Placing his hand on Sabre's shoulder to steady him, he bent a front foot, placed his paw on the table, and observed Sabre's reaction.

With the slow, thorough process, my senses started to revive as I tried to figure out what he was looking for.

Ronnie finally stood up and said, "There are some tests we could run, but I gotta be honest with you. I don't know if they're going to tell us anything this early. Probably they'd only tell us what it's not, and some of the tests have some risks themselves."

"Ronnie, there's one thing I'm sure of. I don't want to put Sabre through any kind of procedure unless the benefits more than outweigh the discomfort. And I know you wouldn't suggest anything that could possibly hurt him." I hesitated, and then added, "What do you think is the strongest possibility?"

"He's acting a lot like it's Degenerative Myelopathy, but I think we ought to wait a little longer and watch him."

"Would I hurt his chances by waiting?"

"Not with what I'm seeing, or more, what I'm *not* seeing."

"What is Degenerative Myelopathy? Ronnie, I've never heard of it."

"It's when the spinal cord starts degenerating. Nobody knows why, or what causes it, but I'm starting to hear of it more and more. It causes paralysis from the rear end first. There's no known cure."

Ronnie stopped speaking, but he was carefully watching my face as the blood drained away and my eyes started to tear. The words "no cure" ricocheted through my head like steel ball bearings thrown at a hundred miles an hour, bouncing against my skull, shredding my fragile veil of hope.

Breathe! I demanded silently, screaming at myself, while my heart raced at the speed of light. I could only hear the rush of blood throbbing in my ears. My breathe came in gasps. The world brightened obscenely into a sudden explosion of yellow that darkened with the threat of turning into black. I thought, *I'm going to pass out!*

Sabre drifted over to me, and tentatively, I released my hold on the table. I knelt beside him, sinking my face into his thick black coat and fighting back tears.

I asked the questions everyone in my position asks. "How long, and what can you do for him?"

I couldn't absorb his answers through my clashing thoughts. His voice merged with other voices I heard drifting in from distant rooms along with the sound of doors opening and closing.

"Every dog is different."

"Months or maybe years."

"Vitamins."

"Regular exercise."

All these words and the other sounds receded into the vague equivalent of a hall of mirrors echoing scattered remnants of useless conversation and disjointed phrases.

I wanted to grab Sabre up in my arms, run away, and take him home with me. I needed time to think.

Ronnie sensed that I was shutting down. He spoke slowly. "We need to wait a little longer, watch him, and bring him back in a couple of weeks."

I managed to nod my agreement, clutching Sabre's fur in desperation until I could get up from the floor.

I left grasping notes about his regimen of vitamins and an appointment for our return, yet my self-control no longer belonged to me. Somehow I drove back home, but I was only going through the motions.

When we came through the garage door, Nissa, as was her practice, sniffed her companion from head to foot. This time, instead of putting up my keys and going on with the usual chores, I stood and watched the two of them, while a sad, lonely feeling melded with fear in the pit of my stomach. Even the familiar welcoming ambiance was absent from our house.

Chapter 26

Gentlemanly Footwear

After meeting with Ronnie, the minutes ticked away like a heated engine left idle to cool. Each insignificant movement, every effort to lift an object from one place to another, required concentration and thought to accomplish. I moved like a person in shock, which was a description very close to the truth. Looking around at my surroundings, what usually made me smile failed to elicit the usual reaction. I knew I couldn't linger in this foggy realm of perfunctory motion, but I felt numb, frozen by a tidal wave that left only paralysis in its wake.

With the agility of someone whose feet are encased in cement, I picked up Sabre's brush and took the dogs out back. His pure enjoyment of being groomed, the affection inherent in the act, finally brought the semblance of a smile to my face; his delight was the key to breaking out of my trance. There were countless factors to consider, and wasting time had no place on the list. I needed to be in motion.

Slowly, Ronnie's advice began to seep into my consciousness in partial thoughts and vague whispers. I began to compose a mental agenda of things to do. Although exercise was a high priority, further wearing down of Sabre's nails was to be avoided because of the possibility of infection. He needed protection from all abrasive surfaces which, in east Dallas, were decidedly unavoidable. Scrounging through the cabinet where I kept brushes, clippers, and other items, I found a role of vet wrap. Sabre was curious when I called him into the kitchen, had him lie down, and started to wrap his back feet. His wagging tail thumped against the floor, his generous, wet kisses swiped across my nose, and the sparkle in his eye told me that he had guessed the game. He was delighted that we were playing "doctor-patient" again. When I picked up the leash, he couldn't contain his excitement. He started to spin. I had trouble attaching the clip to his collar. He plunged through the door almost taking me airborne, stopping only for an exuberant happy dance before charging down the sidewalk.

We only passed a couple of houses when I realized that his hundred pounds with only a thin layer of vet wrap between his foot and the concrete was a losing battle, for the vet wrap as well as for Sabre. I led him across the street to the grassy expanse across from the house. He didn't seem to mind, happily tackling the job of sniffing out the most recent squirrel tracks. There was always something fun to do in Sabre's world.

My next solution was a neoprene webbed version of dog booties from the local pet store chain. While there was improvement, the product was far too expensive, costing $40 and wearing out within half of a block. I started to visualize a leather boot, stitched like a belt, with a sock-like top held on with wide strips of Velcro. Remembering that a friend had given me half of a cowhide, I cut several strips and got out a bottle of glue, hoping for a creation that would last longer and stay on his feet.

The angle of his foot in relation to his leg was not conducive to keeping what is essentially a stiff sock in place for any great distance. The leather easily stood up to the pounding on the cement, but keeping his 'boots' in place was a bigger problem. The frequent stops to readjust became frustrating for Sabre, who didn't want to stop once he got going, and for me, realizing that having to break his pace defeated the purpose of controlled exercise. I was also afraid the looseness would cause him to stumble and fall.

All the large playgrounds at schools in the area posted "No Dogs Allowed" signs. I doubted that the plastic bag in my back pocket would double as a "get out of jail free" card. Our only choice was to stay on the sidewalks. Although the leather was far more durable than the rubber and fabric items we'd tried, no amount of gluing would hold the pieces in place.

By searching the Internet, I found a store close to our house that offered custom-made leather clothing. I vaguely remembered having noticed the store on occasion while driving through Deep Ellum. I called and was referred to Scott, a polite young man who loved dogs.

"I'm calling about my dilemma with a pair of leather boots my dog has to wear to protect his nails from getting infected when his feet drag. He's suffering because no amount of glue will hold them in place!"

"Can you bring Sabre to the store?"

"We'll be there in fifteen or twenty minutes."

I brought the glued boots we'd been using and watched as Scott measured Sabre's leg. He sketched a pattern as he worked, with his figures and notes scattered on the paper in seeming disarray. Sabre had better things to do than to stand and watch. There were shelves to explore and racks of clothing to sniff. More importantly, he had to greet the other employees and allow them to express their adoration. My busy, curious, gregarious German Shepherd was enthusiastically received and made certain that no one was left out of the festivities. I couldn't help but smile as he lapped up the attention and distributed his trademark Sabre kisses.

About a week later, I got a call from Scott to bring Sabre for a fitting. Scott's creations were impressive! The bottoms were thick leather suitable for a heavy belt, yet pliable, unlike the soles of shoes. The layers were held together with metal brads. The top part was a soft, thinner sock, stitched to the underside to prevent sliding or bunching. Snugness was accomplished by a wide band of Velcro at the top that would not cut off circulation while still holding the boot in place.

I learned that day that my faithful companion was also a bit of a show-off. He clopped from person to person, wearing his boots proudly, and patiently allowing Scott to make adjustments. I was pleasantly surprised that all he charged was $23, about half the price of the failed commercial products.

Whether Sabre was the best dressed canine on the block may be debatable, but Platypus Cat now had advanced warning of our approach. The noise we made traveling the city sidewalks resembled a horse traversing a covered wooden bridge, loudly announcing our presence to the napping felines.

Sabre in June 2009, about a month before I lost him. Although the muscles in his back legs had begun to atrophy, he was still able to run and play.

Chapter 27

Home Décor

The next problem to solve was safety in the house. I had never considered the number of obstacles existing within the comfortable confines of home. I walked through the rooms, compiling a mental agenda of what needed to be changed or guarded against. In addition to the entryways, the thresholds between rooms protruded just enough to catch Sabre's nails. I rolled strips of duct tape to fill the gaps and covered them with additional strips. Now, when his nails struck, they would land on soft surfaces.

The house started to resemble a prime example of "Decorating Tips to Make the World Think You've Gone Insane." I was reminded of a show I'd watched on television about a man who covered his walls and windows with aluminum foil to keep aliens from accessing his thoughts. The odd décor didn't matter. What was important, to the exception of all other concerns, was keeping Sabre from any harm that I could prevent. He seemed to appreciate my efforts, watching as I worked, wagging his tail with approval, reaching out to bestow a Sabre kiss on my ear.

Living with German Shepherds was equivalent to sharing space with an ardent admirer. Sound caused by the slightest movement immediately prompted a reaction. They anticipated my next move even before my thoughts became conscious. Sometimes, I thought that Sabre was able to hear me blink. Especially in the mornings when I first woke, he was at my bedside, his face no more than a few inches away, tail thumping rhythmically on the armoire, ready to start the day.

This dance of living spirits wasn't a one-way street with only one of us adjusting to the other. I usually got up before sunrise. The sudden shock of turning on lamps never appealed to me, so I learned to navigate the ambient lighting by touch and memory, making the best of limited vision. Sabre, wanting to be close, followed me and, convinced I might not come back right away, settled where he could see me when I moved again. After a few instances of almost falling over him, I had learned to slow my pace or even stop to determine if the large dark hump in the floor was my furry companion. I carefully stepped around him, and he learned not pick the places where I might walk.

Hard or slippery surfaces throughout the house now needed to be corrected. I bought area rugs and runners to help him on the travertine floor that ran through the entry, hall, and kitchen. I placed the supplemental carpeting to provide pathways between the rooms, being careful to leave out his favorite places where the coolness of the stone felt good on his belly when he napped. I replaced the floor speakers in the living room with smaller ones mounted on the walls.

Satisfied with my improvements for the moment, I stopped to assess the results. My thoughts encompassed a transient speculation that, thus far, I was only beginning to hear the dreadful Degenerative Myelopathy music. I had yet to enter the dance floor.

Chapter 28
Who is Jack Flash?

As long as I stayed busy, I could pretend that nothing was changing, that somehow, what was ahead could be averted. In the early hours of the morning, when most people are still sleeping, I used the time to finish projects for work, play silly games on the computer, read books, or devise projects for fun or to share with friends.

I realized one morning that insulating my feelings was robbing Sabre as unfairly as if I threw his food away and bought the cheapest brand I could find. I sensed in that moment that while some problems were relatively easy to solve at this point, he would soon need so much more from me. I owed it to him to be prepared. The gift of those extra hours was committed to learning as much as I could about Degenerative Myelopathy, which I soon learned was called "DM."

The first site I found in my Internet search was listed under the name of the disease, and among the choices beneath the title were the elements of diagnosis, incidence, research, and treatment. There was information about a support group. My background in psychology and counseling caused immediate interest. I opened the website and began reading. Ronnie's words came back intermittently as I read, but I became somewhat impatient with all the technical descriptions. As I scrolled through the paragraphs, I started to feel overwhelmed by the medical language, details of nutritional requirements and vitamins, and the sheer volume of information. Although the facts would be valuable later, I realized I just wanted to be told what to expect and what to do in plain everyday language.

A little lower on the page I found "A Testament to the Treatment of DM by Jack Flash." I wondered, *Who is Jack Flash?* The Rolling Stones' tune, "Jumpin' Jack Flash," immediately popped into my mind. I was intrigued. I clicked on the link and saw the words "Two Hearts."

The muscles in my face and throat began to constrict. I held my breath, tears welling in my eyes, because I knew with all of my being that when Sabre's heart beat, so did mine. As I read the words, I felt the writer was talking to me. As painful as the conclusions were, the feelings of loneliness began to lose some of their sharp edges. I now knew very clearly who "Jack Flash" was.

My next search was for the author, Marjorie Zimmerman, and I sincerely hoped she'd learned to use the computer she'd mentioned. I wanted to know what she had to say. "Welcome to Jack Flash's Home Page" immediately illuminated the darkness of my office with the soft glow emanating from my monitor. I started to explore. Her message was sad yet oddly hopeful. I replaced my mantra of "don't jump to conclusions" with "don't give up." I was so strongly linked to Sabre that giving up was something I knew I could never do.

On September 18, 2008, I registered a user name, keyed in my password, and joined the message boards. The next hours and succeeding mornings were spent reading. I was engrossed, saddened, and yet driven forward by my "need to know." For several days, I was almost late getting out the door to go to work. I studied the photos and smiled at the amusing stories. I was absorbed by the raw emotions, unadorned and displayed without shame or excuse. At times, tears rolled down my face until my eyes blurred too much to be able to see the pages, but I continued. Sadly, I began to learn.

Although I knew that much of what was available on the internet was contrived or deceitful, the stories I read could not be anything less than real. The numbers of people using the site were staggering, and the number of past members even more. My initial expectation was that the information would be about German Shepherds, but more breeds than I would have imagined, including mixed breeds, were counted in the discussions. One thing was very clear: we all loved our dogs and would do anything we could to help them.

Sharing private thoughts on a medium I could not control once the message was sent was a new experience for me. At the same time, the communications were compelling. I determined that these were not people wallowing in self pity. They shared successes, spreading hope in the wake of their comments. No one was subjected to the anonymous judgment so common in blogs and interactive sites I'd viewed previously. As much as was possible for a disease with so much uncertainty, the discussions were factual. There existed, in the words they typed, a considerate interaction designed to soften the difficulties experienced and the emotions that others felt. No one was ignored or treated with disdain for not knowing the answer to a question, and everyone received responses from others who understood the journey.

When the trappings of society are removed, layers of personality are peeled down to the most basic level. What is important isn't the size of a bank account, the number of vehicles in the driveway, or how many bedrooms are in a house. Absent these symbols, the most valuable commodity is human warmth and the members of this discussion forum were rich in terms of human compassion.

Chapter 29

The Marauding Wild Dog Pack

I gradually began to recognize the names of people and their dogs, and everyday life drifted into dulling familiarity. Aside from the newness of the recent décor, the rhythm of each day played out with lulling regularity. Sabre seemed to enjoy his stylish new footwear, but I had yet to experience the sense of discouragement that others described. Everything seemed deceptively the same. I drifted away from checking the Internet discussions regularly and relied only on the e-mail notices I received when comments were added.

Sabre accepted the necessity of his new boots with his customary grace and enjoyed his walks, especially terrorizing Platypus Cat. Nissa continued to bark her objections and whine when we went out the door without her, although she danced around like an excited puppy when I returned to attach the leash to her collar. Instead of a dog with an illness, Sabre seemed healthier from his new diet. His coat, while always shiny, became luxurious from his new food. Walks at a sustained pace rebuilt the muscles especially through his shoulders, but I couldn't see any change in his powerful back legs. His usual demeanor was happy, and he somehow seemed more energetic. Our efforts had also trimmed off the five pounds Ronnie said he needed to loose.

In the meantime, another terror was stalking our neighborhood. Our area had received city designation as an "historical district" and gained an association that published a newsletter. Each month, the information arrived on the doorstep with occasional notices by e-mail. People were complaining that a pack of wild dogs was preying on the cat population apparently for sport. None of the dogs were reported to appear undernourished, so their attacks didn't seem to be a matter of feeding. They targeted any cat in a vulnerable position. They split into groups and attacked from two or three directions at one time, precluding the easy escape of their prey. They were also not afraid to challenge or threaten people out for a walk, especially if accompanied by a dog, regardless of its size. Urgent concern was expressed for children out playing. Even a family cat napping on a front porch wasn't safe. Owners were subjected to the horrifying sight of their beloved pets attacked in front of them, or they later discovered the torn bodies in their own yards.

The time of day didn't seem to matter. The wild dogs were sighted during morning, afternoon, evening, and overnight, which led to speculation that, perhaps, they were living in an abandoned house or being released on purpose.

Calling animal services, especially in a large city, can be a frustrating proposition and Dallas was no different. Attempts to obtain help using the published number resulted in a recorded message stating that the matter would be addressed in the next ten days. Calls to police were referred back to animal services. Even when they were sighted by residents who attempted to follow them, pursuit by individuals was no match for the wild pack of hunters that often divided, and then disappeared. They were becoming bolder with their successful escapades.

Neighbors talked about forming roving patrols to try to find their hiding places, or if they belonged to someone, to find out where they lived. Descriptions of the dogs involved were inexact and varied, complicating any effort to distinguish between the occasional pet that had escaped a back yard or one the wild pack out on the hunt. Size, color, and breed were continually confused in the growing number of reports and, invariably, at least one was always described as a German Shepherd.

Appeals were issued to the City Counsel for help. Fortunately, our neighborhood representative responded, obtaining cooperation from animal services with a designated number for the specific problem, and the promise of immediate response, day or night. However, the pack continued to evade capture.

With the reports of growing confidence by the seemingly unstoppable band, I started to worry about my daily walks with Sabre and Nissa. Although both were large and in good physical condition, I knew neither would be a match for several dogs that intended to attack in a singular effort. Even with my help, neither could prevail.

Refraining from exercising Sabre was not a consideration. At a dog park, I could not accomplish the steady pace required and I didn't really trust other dog owners to be diligent in controlling their pets. Staying on our street didn't seem to be any safer than any other block. Even if I carried a weapon, I couldn't be certain that I wouldn't hit one of my dogs in the fray. I could have transported him to another area for his walks, but that was a problem because Nissa couldn't stay in the truck on warm days and I wasn't willing to leave her unattended. The temporary solution was taking Sabre back to the house, then taking her out separately. Although I didn't mind the added effort, sometimes I got home from work too late. The dilemma kept me somewhat on edge, as reports of wild dog sightings and attacks remained a frequent topic.

I finally had the disturbing opportunity to observe this troublesome pack for myself. I had just gotten out of bed, turned the coffee pot on, and started into my office when Sabre and Nissa started barking with the same intensity usually applied to someone actually on the front porch. I ran to see what had caused the stir, with an uncharacteristic hesitance. I grabbed a flashlight, not only to be able to illuminate what might be outside, but because the heft of the instrument could also double as protection.

I immediately saw through the window what had caused the dogs to become upset. A large dog of indiscriminate breed was exploring, stepping off the sidewalk and into the yard. Another was crossing the street, and two other dogs had already reached the grassy area. The commotion of my two protectors had attracted the attention of the closest one. He stood in the grass, head up, staring pointedly at the three of us. I felt exposed and vulnerable behind the thin panes of glass. The two across the way had turned their gaze in our direction.

Despite their adamant reluctance, I pulled both dogs from the windows and closed them in the back bedroom, their threatening barks morphing into frustrated whines. My heart was beating rapidly and I was seized by icy fingers of fear when I grabbed the telephone and hit the emergency animal control number I had programmed into the register.

I went back to the kitchen, peering out from around the refrigerator to the front yard. Although the other dogs had returned to exploring across the street, the large one was still standing as we had left him, staring into our house as if contemplating his next move. I grabbed the pistol I kept in a drawer for an emergency, holding the handle in one hand with my finger on the housing above the trigger, while I held the phone in my other hand. I reported the description and location of the invaders. I waited until the animal control truck arrived to search, despite my certainty that due to the time needed to get here, they would not be able to find any trace of the vicious pack.

The next day, I sent a polite message to the president of the association urging him to please stop describing the dogs as German Shepherds and attached pictures of German Shepherds with several different views and positions. I then offered a description of size, color, type of ears, and other aspects of the dogs I'd seen. With a more objective characterization, I suggested, the problem of locating them might be more easily solved.

Two or three weeks later, an e-mail arrived reporting that two of the dogs had been captured. Talk of the attacks lessened and soon the fear pervading the neighborhood dissipated. Sabre and Nissa got their daily walk schedule back. Concerns and worry about owned and unowned cats seemed to fade away. I never learned where the wild dogs came from, whether they belonged to someone, or if they were surviving on the streets, but I will never forget their menacing stares that seemed to spring from their ancient instincts.

Sabre didn't know I was watching him. The look in his face shows his misery at his loss of independence and abilities. Courtesy of Marty Mann.

Chapter 30

Calling the Role

Our return to the regular exercise circuit brought relief. I mentally called the roll of neighborhood cats along our way, hoping they'd all survived the scourge. Sabre seemed anxious to cover the ground a little faster than usual. Nissa had alerted us to the fact that Calico was still the reigning queen of her urban jungle. No Tail, her sometimes hunting companion, had been with her earlier in the day. Her court of Yellow Cat, Stripes, Stilts, and all the usual faces were present, lounging on the driveways and porches with their customary looks of disdain as we passed.

When we rounded the block where Platypus Cat lived, I felt a tug of fear, hoping he hadn't mistaken the pack of killers for the blustery but innocuous dogs that would go away if he puffed up, arched his back, and spit at them. My eyes searched the yards as we approached his accustomed domain. Sabre held his head a little higher as if trying to increase his field of view. Our sense of urgency was instantly placated when Platypus Cat rose up from the grass in classic pose, back forming a tighter arch, tail seemingly twice its normal puffiness, his ears flatter against his head than ever before, and a growl that was more greeting than warning. I watched in surprise as Sabre abandoned his cheerfully impertinent invasion of space and executed his happy dance. Our friendship was renewed after a long, anxious absence.

The next corner seized my joy and smashed my fragile hope on the hard, unyielding concrete. Sabre's rear legs crossed, his back end swayed, he stumbled, twisted backwards, and then fell to the sidewalk. A pain unlike any I'd felt before, equal to a flaming arrow, pierced my heart and seared all viable flesh in its path. My vision glazed over, leaving dark jagged edges that obscured my sight. My hiding place had been discovered, exposing me to the reality I'd been trying desperately to avoid. I wanted to crumble to the ground, but somehow I remained upright, as Sabre immediately recovered. He pulled me along with him, as he resumed his course and pace. I tried to choke back the feelings coursing through me to keep them hidden as I remembered the cautions of those in the discussion group. Allowing emotions to surface and take over caused unneeded stress that should not be passed along from human to canine. By the time we reached the front door, tears were rolling uncontrolled down my face.

Nissa's exuberant anticipation of her walk saved me. Taking her out would give me the time I needed to regain composure and control. I quickly released the clip from Sabre's collar, placing the shiny metal in the loop on hers. At that precise moment, I looked into Sabre's eyes. His attention was focused on me, and his tail was wagging behind him, a gently swaying motion that was oddly reassuring. I held the center of his gaze for what I thought was just a second too long. Inexplicably, I felt a calmness I knew I didn't own, but that somehow became mine as I reluctantly pulled my eyes away and walked out the door.

Later when we returned, I had no memory of our excursion, but Nissa bounded through the doorway, having explored the sights and smells she'd been missing. She headed for Sabre without her standard detour by the feeding mat. Her usual pattern was to check for the magic appearance of her dinner while she was gone. Sabre licked her face, then she sidled over to the water bowl. I stood in place as if my feet had been glued to the floor.

Sabre seemed tired but happy, and the expression on his face was placid and tranquil. Nissa's usual anticipation of the approaching dinner hour was somewhat muted as she resumed her position of vigil at the window. My senses were numbed.

The roller coaster ride of emotions from the previous hour played into an indistinguishable collage of misshaped thoughts and remnants of the pain I'd experienced. For the first time in all the years we'd lived there, I felt lost inside our home, as if a guarded secret had been spoken out loud, irrevocably transforming its character and composition, leaving in the wake of exposure an unsettling certainty.

Chapter 31

A New Puppy Next Door

The next few days seemed as if I was looking at the world through the wrong end of a telescope. Every thought began and ended with a question.

I returned to the information I'd been too impatient to read before, trying to absorb the vagaries that DM presented. I thoroughly researched the archives of Jack Flash's website and then scoured the discussion forums for anything that could potentially explain or clarify. Whereas before, I'd avoided forming the words in my mind, as if not speaking the name would prevent the disease from gaining power. Now, I became a sponge soaking up all things DM.

I resumed my Internet search with increased dedication, certain there would be a wealth of information and studies I could read, facts I could glean. Admittedly, I was looking for that miracle that would exorcize the phantom. The offerings were meager; only a few researchers were associated with the topic. I assumed the disease had been recently discovered, however, that didn't bear out unless 1973 could be considered recent. Only a lone scientist in Florida seemed to have dedicated his life's work to the complexities of treatment. All the others appeared for a brief moment, short beginnings with too many miles yet to travel. The only wealth of information was the one I'd already found.

Burglars know that a single loud noise, followed by silence, will cause people to dismiss what they have heard, leaving the criminals free to pursue their purpose. By definition, DM is a burglar that creeps in with the practiced silence of an invisible thief. Though an indelible mark may be left behind after a disturbing incident, the intermittent appearance of any symptoms causes the observer to doubt what was witnessed.

Sabre approached each day as a new adventure. He showed none of the stress I was feeling, and he seemed to consider his journey through the neighborhood as an opportunity for adding to his growing list of friends. The two young girls in the house next to us had often watched us pass during our walks. Although they shied away, they were unable to keep their eyes off of this imposing beast that lived next door. Sabre, however, seemed to sense the exact moment that their interest exceeded their fear. He hesitated where their sidewalk crossed the city walkway, wagging his tail and looking up at the porch where they were sitting on the steps. For a moment, they watched us as we gazed at them.

I broke the silence. "Would you like to pet him?" Their eyes grew wide with both anticipation and fear. I assured them, "He doesn't bite and he won't hurt you, but he'll probably want to give you a kiss."

Emphasizing my words, Sabre sat and brushed his tail over the ground in a silent, friendly invitation. He absorbed their attention with his usual delight.

While her sister reached out to stroke his head, the younger one was more tentative and hesitant to reach out, most likely because he was twice her size. Her courage grew through her sister's success, and she reached out, barely touching him. At the moment of contact, she instantly drew her hand away, overcome with squeals of laughter. Soon they were competing to run their hands over his lush coat, feel the softness of his ears, and giggle at his kisses.

Greeting the girls next door became a part of our walks. Not long after the day they met, I heard the excited yips of a new puppy next door. His new friends were occupied now, but Sabre didn't seem to mind. He had fulfilled his role of ambassador and had other goals to accomplish.

Chapter 32

Eating Dirt

We attracted attention in the neighborhood as we walked along the streets. Sabre's clomping boots beat out a unique rhythm in advance of the most likely humorous sight of me racing to keep up. Except for his fancy footwear, we looked like anyone else out for an afternoon jaunt. People we never met began to call out greetings as we passed. Often, they stopped to talk, especially those who were also out with their dogs. The most recurrent conversational opening was the reason for his wearing the boots.

While keeping up our pace was important, I also believed there were valid reasons to stop and talk to people. I tried to explain DM to them. I can't remember anyone we chatted with who had heard of the disease that was slowly taking command of our life. Comprehension was difficult and confusion invariably showed in their faces and comments. Sabre looked so normal, healthy, and happy that they had trouble believing he was sick. Without exception, each conversation dissolved into uncomfortable silence. I knew the question they wanted to ask but were reluctant to voice: "How long?"

I gave them the only answers I knew to the unasked question. "It isn't painful," I was careful to say. "The progression goes from a loss of sensations to the loss of the ability to stand, to walk. There's no cure, but each dog progresses at a different rate."

As weeks and months passed, the inevitable clippety cloppety sound of our treks along the sidewalks brought greetings and smiles, along with continued careful observation from those we encountered. They remembered Sabre's name, and his ears perked up with recognition when they beckoned him. Sabre continued to add members to his fan club. I returned from our jaunts with a special pride in this marvelous creature that I loved. Yet my heart grew heavy at the same time with the realization that we were stalked by something I couldn't fix, a despicable force that would inevitably defeat us both.

Everyone needs an emotional outlet, someone whose caring is unquestioned, or someone with whom anything can be said or discussed. Sabre had always been my confidant. A slight, most likely unintended by a friend, a particularly difficult episode with a client, an argument that couldn't be easily resolved, a painful knowledge that hurt deep inside, were the things I told him. I talked through my dilemmas with my most faithful friend, his gentle eyes always portraying that he was on my side, right or wrong. DM was the only topic off limits. How could I talk to him about him?

His stumbling became more frequent, and crossing his back legs over became more pronounced. To keep things light, I told him, "You're getting to be an old drunk. You need to lay off the sauce and quit sneaking into the liquor cabinet when I'm asleep."

I watched his expressions, seeing only brief confusion and then immediate recovery as he figured out my joke and continued on his way otherwise unaffected.

Staying upbeat and completely ignoring the gravity of the changes in his world seemed deceptive and unfair. I struggled to find a way to join our reality with the more important commitment that had always been present. Sabre was the German Shepherd dog I had always dreamed of, everything I'd always wanted, and the love I felt for him defied explanation or description. As I would have done with any other friend, I decided I would tell him the truth, assuring him that I would never abandon him, that I would do anything and everything he needed. He looked into my heart and mind with his deep, soulful eyes, his gaze convincing me that he somehow understood. During those moments, the bond between us strengthened in ways I'd never have believed possible. I glanced over at Nissa to see her watching us, physically apart, yet equally important. I called her over to us.

Strangely around this time, Sabre started eating dirt. At first, I was upset, thinking his bewildering practice could be harmful. I had heard of people all over the world guarding their "dirt finds," sneaking off into the woods to their treasured deposits of red clay, defying reason, and persisting against the caution of doctors. Perhaps the habit rose from some instinctive clue for dogs, as well as humans. Speculation was that those who chose this perceived delicacy were deficient in iron. Another explanation was that eating dirt removed poisonous substances from the body and reduced toxins acquired through the process of living. Since DM is considered an autoimmune disease, I thought that Sabre, perceiving the changes he was going through, sensed the difference within his body. Ronnie expressed no concern when I mentioned eating dirt, so I stopped worrying and was amused, especially when I noticed that Nissa had also acquired the taste. I guessed she figured Sabre knew best.

Chapter 33

A Dog's Got to Look Good

While the routines of life continued to feel the same, I could discern subtle changes in Sabre's behavior. He'd always insisted on accompanying guests to our rest room. He had a captive audience, and they had the opportunity to pet him. Saying no simply wasn't an option he afforded. If they closed the door, his nose thwarted their effort. Privacy was of no concern to him. I noticed, however, that when he backed away, he hesitated and threw his weight in the direction he wanted to go, as he retreated to another room.

Lying down was no longer the smooth, graceful motion as before. Getting up was more difficult, as well, requiring him to dig his front nails into the carpet for stability and hunch forward to reduce the weight on his rear legs. Rising from harder surfaces required him to quickly thrust his weight forward and shift his back legs underneath in a rapid, continuous motion to keep from falling back.

Each time I saw him adjust sent a stab of pain through me. He didn't seem to notice. He never whimpered or showed any indication of discomfort or complaint. Sabre coped with the difficulties. While I wanted to fall apart, I could not allow emotion to defeat my ability to care for him.

I began to change routines. Sabre had always loved to be brushed, walking along with the motion of the strokes and returning to the starting point to feel the marvelous sensations again and again. I started bringing the brush with me to his place on the floor, rubbing his ears and caressing his head, as I whisked the brush through his coat. I could see the gratitude in his eyes, his enjoyment not only of the attention, but his appreciation of the gift that preserved the pleasurable experience he loved. As I talked to him, he lifted his head to lick my hand. Sometimes, Nissa took her place beside us, and I reached out to pull her close. Those moments grew and magnified in meaning; a minute wasn't a minute, the culmination of measurable seconds. Time could no longer be defined in the usual ways, but became something far more precious, a communication unrestricted by definable limitations.

Exercise was crucial to keep the strength left in his muscles and his general health, but as his stamina diminished, our daily walks gave way to walks every other day. Regardless of temperature or rain, we walked. His leather boots, with the soft leather sock sewn in, kept his feet dry. On Ronnie's advice, I rubbed zinc oxide ointment into his pads when we returned to keep them from drying out.

Sabre accepted the changes with his customary graciousness. His attitude stayed upbeat, and his expressions remained trusting. I soon realized that his strength was feeding mine.

Chapter 34
A Nose for Diagnostics

Dogs are famous for using their noses. I've often seen videos that show them along highways during traffic stops and in the hallways of schools searching for drugs. The phenomenon has become a normal sight, an expectation hardly worthy of notice. News broadcasts are full of accounts of the large quantities found by dogs that people would likely not have discovered or taken considerably more time to locate.

Television reports include their abilities to locate explosives in airports and war zones. I read an article that described the official use of canines in formal diagnosis with accounts of their uncanny accuracy. I often joked about my two lazy boarders needing to get out and find a job to help support their food habit. I again threatened to spray their tails with Pledge and make them dust. At least, I reasoned, they could help with the chores. I then added careers in law enforcement to round out my rant. In unison, they looked at me, suppressing their urge to yawn in boredom, pretending they couldn't decipher the noise coming from my direction.

Sabre had another use for his nose. Invariably, he was the first sight I became aware of each time I stepped out of the shower. He positioned himself between the sinks at the junction of the bath area and my bedroom. The moment I emerged, his nose began working overtime. A significant degree of dexterity was required on my part to be able to dress and, especially when the weather was cold, avoid the shock of a cold wet nose on exposed skin. Sabre didn't mind if I shrieked; the extra bonus seemed only to add to his game. He had determined that humans smell best just after a shower, and he was determined not to miss the experience.

Nissa apparently thought the game we played of sniff and

dodge was beneath her. With obvious disgust and an occasional snort for emphasis, she would remove herself from the meaningless frivolity and go off to another room, no doubt checking the clock to determine the exact number of minutes and hours until dinnertime.

Nissa may have lacked the verbal ability to express what she sensed, but her behavior revealed that she knew something was terribly wrong with Sabre. I glanced up from working and reading and saw her watching when Sabre had trouble getting up. Sometimes, she walked over to where he was lying and carefully sniffed his body from head to tail.

Her behavior was significant, having once observed Sabre doing the same thing with a friend who had come to visit. During one of our Saturday morning chats, we had steaming cups of coffee in front of us, coffee cake at the center of the kitchen table, and plates and forks within reach. Sabre kept returning to carefully and diligently sniff at her right side. Our first thought was that something had spilled on her blouse, but there was nothing to indicate that had happened. His persistence, however, was hard to dismiss.

When asked, he reluctantly moved away and found a place to lie down, although staying within sight of his target. Eventually, he returned to sniff, sat back and looked up at her face. He slowly wagged his tail and delivered his unspoken message. Finding no apparent reason for his unusual attention, we shrugged has actions off and continued to enjoy our discussions. A few days later, I received a call from the hospital. My friend relayed the news of a successful appendectomy. She had called to thank Sabre for his early diagnosis. In that moment, his actions suddenly made sense.

Chapter 35

Silent Morning

If asked to choose the time of the day I loved the best, I would name the early hours of morning without any hesitation. Each day began with the rhythm of Sabre's tail against the armoire, the expectant look on his face my first sight of the day, with the glow from the night light reflecting in his eyes. From the time he first knew that he finally owned a human, and every day after that, he was my alarm clock of pure joy, a combination of patience and anticipation as I awakened. Nissa hung back from the door as the ritual played out, most likely to be closer to the Milk-Bones. Nissa loved food, any kind and any time.

The two of them enthusiastically chomped away at their treats, and Nissa slipped in behind Sabre to make sure that no crumbs remained behind. Then, they galloped to the back door to go out, accompanied by the chugging sounds of the coffee pot that heralded my morning treat, the perfect beginning to any day. Invariably, they came back in and abandoned me to my own devices while they went back to sleep, one on either side of my chair as I checked the computer for unanswered e-mails, or tackled the latest project.

Sometimes, I listened to music and played games, as dawn slowly graced the sky in buoyant solitude and a sense of peacefulness. Those quiet times of day belied the disruptions the remaining hours held, creating the illusion of a sanctuary from life's cuts and bruises. I sensed, however, that something was missing that I couldn't quite discern. My usual feelings of calm and contentment gave way to a gnawing angst that refused to go away, tugged at my concentration, and replaced with apprehension that threatened to grow into panic.

I wandered through the house, staring out the front windows, searching for a cause, but finding nothing. My awareness finally took material form with an icy, desolate start, when I realized that I hadn't heard the thumping of Sabre's tail. I took both dogs out to the back yard, allowing Sabre to reach the midway point before calling him to me. He knew there would be a good reason for me calling him, and I didn't disappoint him. I knelt in front, wrapped my arms around his neck, whispered that he was a good boy, and felt the familiar Sabre kisses in my ear and the burning trail of tears on my cheeks. His tail hung on the ground, doubling back slightly, unmoving and lifeless. He would never again be able to wag his happy tail.

I walked back into the house as far as I could get from the back door, leaving Sabre and Nissa to search the yard for signs of intruders and bark at imaginary dangers in the alley. I couldn't allow my tightly swirling emotions to unfurl. Sabre's sensitivity would not fail to miss the emotions I felt. He didn't deserve the disease, much less to absorb the jagged infusion of negativity. My tears soon dried, expelled from consciousness by anger, and my rage took on a physical dimension, finally reaching a crescendo that left me weak and drained. I sank to the floor, tears once again streaming down my face, streaking rapidly, unstoppable. I felt helpless and furious that life could be so unfair to such a beautiful spirit.

I sat there on the floor for several moments, staring out the window without seeing, unable to command my thoughts, willing my control to return. Life was redefined in that one moment and forever changed. There could be no turning back.

Chapter 36

Dangling Conversations

My attention was now divided between the rough sidewalks with their inherent pitfalls and Sabre's tail getting tangled in his back legs as he walked, causing him to fall. Neighbors called out their greetings as before, but slower, more hesitant, as they watched his wobbly progress. Sabre, however, was dauntless, showing no concern for his instability. His indomitable spirit, an indelible aura of jubilation, burst through in his acknowledgment of each member of his neighborhood fan club. For Sabre, nothing was different. No one was deprived of a Sabre kiss. Only the children seemed able to match his exuberance.

Some folks crossed the street to talk to us. Often, those who drove by slowed down and stopped. Their questions became more direct although reluctant. I expanded my explanation of the process of degeneration of his spine that caused him to lose sensation, and, subsequently, his muscular control. Without nerves to function, muscles stopped working, and coordination and strength was lost. Invariably conversations dwindled away to nothingness. Although the disease was not painful in ways that would normally be expected, the pervasive sense of loss and helplessness was unmistakable.

People do care about others, even those who are basically strangers, yet there are no rules to follow about how to respond to the pain that foretells of impending sorrow. The lump in my throat hampered my ability to speak, simultaneously diminishing the ability of other people to respond. The sadness that I failed to hide was pervasive, no matter how cheerful I tried to be. Often, I watched them walk away as they stifled the urge to look back. I was reminded of Simon and Garfunkle's song "Dangling Conversations." That title repeated in my mind along with a lonely feeling.

As the weeks passed, they no longer stopped to chat, only smiling and waving as they drove by. They didn't cross the street as before, instead calling out their greetings from a distance. Even among those we knew as friends, exchanges became shorter and increasingly awkward. Kindness prompted them to ask how we were doing, but explanations were too painful for them to hear. I started keeping my replies short with a renewed commitment to act is if nothing was wrong. I could read the confusion on their faces at the contradictions between what they heard and what they saw.

Sabre looked bright and healthy. His expressions were animated and vied with their ability to understand the answers. Yet, looking down at him and gazing into his wise eyes, my resolve seemed to strengthen. His courage kindled a fire in me to follow his example, to be stronger than I perceived myself to be.

One Sunday morning, he was especially energetic as he lay on his side on the kitchen floor, hardly able to keep from moving, making the process of securing the Velcro straps on his boots difficult at best. Nissa bounced from window to window, alternating between barks of protest and pleading whines as we walked out the door and raced off down the sidewalk. The cats scattered from their comfortable positions on driveways and lawns with their customary disgust as Sabre delighted in his pretense of "the mighty hunter."

The hour was later than usual, and people were out taking care of weekend chores. Sabre was excited and anxious to get on with his jaunt, so I didn't stop to talk with anyone. I called out greetings, but kept my focus on the path ahead. Our only stops were for Sabre to leave his calling card on telephone posts and trees and to investigate particularly interesting smells. His happiness was infectious. I couldn't help but smile at his playful approach to what would have been, for a human, boring through repetition.

As we rounded the corner of the next block, a dog I'd never seen came bounding across the street toward us. I was immediately frightened, unable to read his intent and fearful that the intense interest could accelerate into aggression. I knew that Sabre couldn't defend himself. There was nothing I could do to halt the approach. The dog trotted out from a driveway gate at the side of a house. This was not a matter of oversight or a latch that hadn't caught. The gate was standing wide open, and the owner was nowhere to be seen.

I wrapped my arms around Sabre to protect him, and I started yelling, "Hey! Come get your dog, please! Whoever owns this dog, please, come get him!"

For several excruciating minutes, no one responded. I looked around for anything I could use to ward off the unwanted encounter, hoping for a stick, a rock, anything I could use to thwart the dog's steady advance, but there was nothing.

As the dog neared, I held Sabre tighter to shield him and kept one arm free to fight back. I again screamed, "Come get your dog!"

Fearing that my own terror would incite the unknown canine, I switched to a voice that I hoped would carry the power of command.

"Sit!" No response. "Down!" I was ignored. The dog was focused on Sabre, and nothing I shouted made any difference. Exasperated, I screamed as loud as I could, "Stop!"

I knew that dogs can sense when another dog is weak and that triggered their instinct to attack. I watched for fur rising on its back, ears pricking forward, eyes locked, any indication of aggression. Although I could detect no signs, my fear magnified.

I yelled again in desperation, "Come get your damned dog!"

The owner finally peaked around the corner through the gate. "Ranger—*here!*" he called.

The distraction only slightly slowed the dog's advance.

"Ranger, get back here!" The dog stopped, but continued staring at Sabre, until the owner caught up and grabbed his collar.

Then, the man simply turned and walked back to his house with his hand on his dog's collar. He offered not a single world of apology.

I was shaking, as the scene played over in my mind. Sweat ran down my face and into my eyes. At that moment, I got mad. I was furious that he had failed to keep his dog under control and ignored my frantic attempt to keep Sabre from harm. The man showed no concern that my dog was crippled.

Sabre watched me with a look of understanding on his face. I didn't know if his leaning against me and kissing my face was gratitude or reassurance. I held him closer to me, trying to stifle the pervading sense of guilt that I had failed to protect him.

We continued toward the end of the block and Sabre apparently forgot the incident, but I could not. I took Nissa in a different direction for her walk. Forcing myself to breathe deeply, I tried to calm my emotions that were still raging, but the traces of fear and helplessness remained, coupled with a primitive urge to go back to the man's house and pour out my aggression on the cause of my distress.

Chapter 37
Nissa's Purple Fantasy

We continued a regular pattern of exercise, but I always scanned the gate belonging to our inconsiderate neighbor each time we approached the corner. I was wary of a repeat event that might not turn out as well the second time.

Since Sabre was only able to go for walks every other day, the added effort of compensating for the lack of strength in his back legs made his front legs tire and used up his store of energy. Days in between were for rest. Again, he offered no complaint and took each change in his stride. I was continually amazed at his ability to cope. His willing, always grateful personality never changed, and his excitement over the anticipated strolls never dampened.

Other maneuvers required invention on his part to accomplish what had once been easy. In tight spaces that required him to back away, I watched him adjust his stance, hesitate as if thinking through the next move, then balance his weight and thrust his front legs forward in a surprisingly smooth motion. With careful maneuvering, he was able to head in the direction of his choosing without faltering.

The soles of his thick leather boots had become tattered around the edges, and the metal brads, once shiny and new, wore down and almost ground away to the point that only the posts holding the two pieces of leather together remained. The time had arrived for a new pair of boots.

I called Scott, and we had a new pair within days. The combination of hard leather on the outside and the soft leather sock inside had given him six months of comfortable protection. With the carpet runners inside the house, duct tape on all the entries, and the boots for exercise, the tops of his nails had escaped the typical wearing down caused by DM.

They never abraded to the point of bleeding, and the risk of infection had been averted.

All of the physical difficulties he lived with had no effect on his delight at seeing special friends. I had noticed over the years that Sabre seemed to compartmentalize the humans in his life. Some were fun for the hours they entered his domain, but others held a special place. He greeted them differently, remaining closer instead of wandering off to avoid the inevitable droning of human conversation.

We soon learned that Tammy, a long-time friend, would be visiting for a few days, and the welcomed news brought a sense of excitement. My canine housekeeping police diligently supervised the preparations for our guest, watching to make sure I performed adequately. Nissa, too, shared Sabre's special enjoyment whenever Tammy came through the door, and they both rushed around her. Sabre kissed her hand, and Nissa skittered around in circles yipping and swirling as close as possible for the attention of this person they both adored. That they remembered her from visit to visit, no matter how many months or years apart, was never in doubt.

Nissa idolized Tammy. Although sweet and affectionate with every visitor, she paid minimal attention after saying hello and quickly reverted to her job of watching through the front windows for cats, dogs, and squirrels during ensuing conversations. In Tammy's presence, she jubilantly upstaged Sabre. She seemed to emulate Tammy by carefully observing her slightest movements, following her through the house, and lying down as close as possible. If a dog can imitate the affectations of a person, Nissa certainly succeeded where Tammy was concerned. She took on airs of uncharacteristic sophistication, holding her head up in a dignified fashion, seeming more mature and less puppy-like. Her demeanor bordered on a sophistication that belied her happy, carefree disposition. Nissa was, indeed, smitten.

The occasion was a dual purpose event, part business, the attendance of a professional conference, and part fun, spending time together in the pleasurable pursuit of catching up between friends. As we left each morning to drive to the hospital where the event was being held, Nissa charged the door trying to edge through the opening to accompany us. We giggled as the door closed behind us and Nissa barked her displeasure at being left behind in a single, yet definitive yip. The same pattern was repeated when Nissa apparently sensed that I was leaving again to pick up her special friend in the afternoons.

Coming through the door on our return, Nissa danced around Tammy as if she had just arrived. Even Sabre eyed her unusual behavior. Clothes changed, dinner behind us, Nissa rushed to the couch to sit by Tammy.

Tammy's visit came to an end too soon, I'm sure, for Nissa. In the days that followed, Nissa discovered what would become her most prized possession. Tammy had forgotten a part of her wardrobe when we'd combined a load of wash. Returning home from work the next day, I concluded that Nissa had rummaged around in the unfolded clothing on top of the dryer. Probably standing on her back legs, she had managed to pull a pair of lavender panties from the pile. She immediately claimed them as her own. She never attempted to tear them up. Instead, she carried them from room to room, happily nestling with them between her front paws even when she stood vigil at the windows. When she went to sleep, she contentedly curled up around them, dreaming the enchantments in a happy little girl's fantasies.

I tried to put them on one of her stuffed toys, she haughtily resisted my attempts to disguise the object of her affection, pulling them off with a disgusted snort. She insisted on carrying them around with her. I finally gave up. I simply smiled at the looks of surprise on the faces of the visitors who came after. Nissa was happy, and that was the important thing.

Chapter 38

Harmony in Discord

Sabre's constant good spirits and his willingness to handle anything that came his way sparked creativity in compensating for his losses in mobility. Reluctant to deprive him of the pleasures he'd always appreciated, I began devising new ways of meeting his needs.

Frequent belly rubs were a favorite pastime. He turned on his side, his snorts of pleasure bringing smiles and laughter. Nissa came running to see what she was missing, hoping, for a Milk-Bone or some other tidbit. She seemed to absorb the significance of the exchange, nestling close beside us, her brown eyes watching intently.

Time passed without definition, carrying no importance, whether for a few minutes, or an hour, outweighing all other considerations. Briefly, the emotional pain that came with DM edged out of my mind. We became even closer, more than I could have ever believed possible. I didn't feel the cool stone floors pressing into my knees, and the strained muscles in my back whispered only a brief complaint before vanishing like a tiny breeze disappearing into the distance. I never tired or lost my concentration on my two gentle spirits. I felt calm and peaceful within those moments.

Brushing progressed to massages. Starting with his feet, and working up his legs and the spaces in his spine, I gently stroked his muscles, hoping in some small way to stimulate the fading nerves. Unconsciously, I suppose I was bargaining for responses that were not likely to come. Sometimes, his leg would jerk, and I couldn't help but hope that a nerve had responded to the touch. I knew, more likely, the reaction was involuntary. Yet even that almost certain knowledge failed to diminish the magic and contentment of those special moments that transformed all concerns and worries into a celebration of the relationship we shared.

Strangely, one evening, I noticed that my hands felt hotter than usual, pulsating with increasing warmth that radiated through my fingers. Concerned that Sabre might have a fever, I felt his nose with my arm, but found only a cool wetness. Thinking the sensation was my imagination, I tested my hand against my other arm. The heat coursing through them was undeniable and equally unexplainable. As I continued to massage his body, I studied him. His breathing was even, mimicking the slow rhythm of sleep. His eyes were open but appeared glazed. Nissa, too, seemed mesmerized. Her head and body leaned in his direction, her eyes darker, the slow motion of air seeping in and flowing out bringing an almost indiscernible rise and fall to her chest.

I worked my way to his shoulders, his neck, then the top of his head, watching him in fascination, and glancing at the serene expression on Nissa's face. Sabre was still and quiet, his breathing hardly registering. Nissa hardly seemed to blink as she remained entranced by the scene playing out in front of her. My own breathing was akin to the regularity of sleep, but somewhat slower, reaching the fullest depths of my lungs. While my muscles had unknowingly relaxed, the tension had also dissipated, remarkable only through its marked absence. Only the heat in my hands remained, the source unknown without conscious control. Slowly, they returned to their normal temperature.

Neither dog moved when I got up. I didn't even bother to make coffee for the next morning. The veil of sleepiness held off just long enough for me to reach my bed and pull the covers over me as I fell into the deep trance of slumber, unaware that my head had even touched my pillow.

Chapter 39

The Quiet Hours of Morning

Time is marked by milestones; the events that pierce our surface consciousness define harmony or discord through their significance at the depths of who we are. We assign importance to dates in our lives, sweet sixteen, turning twenty-one, graduations, wedding vows, all those acts meant to preserve the rewards of individual experience. The harsh, painful events also seem to find their place, as if written with indelible ink. Those, too, are etched into our sub-conscious mind, preserved without our permission. No matter how much we want to shut them out, those memories become a part of us. While they may diminish or fade over time, they are never forgotten.

My saddest morning was the first time when Sabre didn't appear at my bedside when I opened my eyes. At first, I thought the hour was too early for us to get up, but immediately dismissed that explanation. No hour of the night or day had ever been too soon to begin a new day. Sabre's happy face, only inches from mine, had made owning an alarm clock unnecessary from the beginning of his life with me. His enthusiastic greetings had imbued my days with cheerfulness.

I looked through the door to the place he usually claimed for sleep. His eyes found mine with a look that almost seemed to be an apology, as if, somehow, he thought he had failed me. He wanted to be in his chosen place when I awakened. I moved swiftly to his side.

"It's not your fault, baby boy," I crooned, trying desperately, without success, to hold back a volcano of emotion that threatened to overcome my self-control.

All the advice I'd read on the discussion list to remain upbeat and not allow negative feelings to show vanished instantly, as breathing came in desperate gasps and tears blurred my vision. My arms around his neck, I held onto him the way a drowning person clings to a piece of driftwood in the struggle to survive.

Sabre remained still, as I buried my face in the soft fur of his neck. I held on until, eventually, my tears dried and my breathing started to return to normal. My clinched hands released their grip on his coat. Sabre turned his head and kissed my face, starting with my cheek and following through to my ear. The tickling kiss allowed a stifled laugh to escape into the silent room. Nissa had appeared from around the corner to add her affection. Soon, we were rolling on the floor, Nissa yipping, me laughing, and Sabre aiming kisses that often landed in empty air.

The free fall of tears had released the tension that had built from holding back, lifting our spirits. I realized that honesty was as much a part of living with DM as constant vigilance and control of emotion. From that day forward, when I awakened, I went to him, comfortable again with preserving the upbeat attitude that was important as this insidious disease progressed. I had learned that my responsibility to him didn't require ignoring his falls or his disabilities. My role was reaching out to him through his stumbling with words of encouragement and an acknowledgment that when he fell, I would there for him. Once again, the bond between us gained new dimensions.

Chapter 40
Life of Simple Pleasures

I rescheduled that day's appointments. Leaving Sabre didn't feel right. I sensed that time together was what we all needed. Closeness and caring were of greater magnitude than anything that could be done on another day. Before I could bring his Milk Bone to him, he had dragged his unwilling body to the door into the kitchen. His usual eager expression was restored, and his face and eyes said his manner of travel didn't matter.

For me, the morning's event was momentous, but Sabre simply coped with yet another alteration. Sometimes the sparkle in his eyes made me think he believed that one day I'd fix this affliction and life would be as before. He knew I'd fixed his tail with warms soaks, medicine, and time. When he got the fungus on his ears where I'd taken him for grooming, I'd also fixed that with the healing solution provided by Ronnie. A little more time was all he apparently thought I needed to fix the disease that robbed him of his independence.

DM was an accumulation of sporadic surprises. One day, he was unable to crawl from place to place. The next day, he took several steps at his old pace, almost appearing normal. Our walks became infrequent, yet sometimes when I thought we should go home, he wanted to keep on going. His patient, trusting demeanor never changed.

As much as I wanted to deny the reality ahead of us, I knew I had to start to prepare for a day I never wanted to endure. I talked to Ronnie, extracting his promise that when that day came, he would come to the house. When the time arrived to part with my companion, Sabre would be comfortable and secure in the home he loved, with Nissa and me at this side, love holding him close to us.

When I could find the courage, I read sections on the

discussion list devoted to preparing for the final stages. I used the early hours after their breakfast when both dogs had gone back to napping. My vow to Sabre was that I would heed the signs. I would not allow him to languish in misery because of my own need to keep him with me. If life could not have quality and his days reached the point of holding no joy in the expectation of the one to follow, I would let him go.

During the quiet hours of solitude, when there was no one else to reach out to, I wrote my thoughts. Without fail, the concerned and caring responses of those who had walked the path we were traveling always appeared. The lonely hours yielded understanding from those who knew the feelings I struggled with. They had traveled my same journey. Under Sabre's watchful eye, I couldn't allow my emotions to rule. Through my keyboard and the kindness of strangers, I found an outlet that shored up my strength.

Chapter 41
Stolen Thunder

Although Sabre had never been a dog that particularly enjoyed playing fetch, a new toy sparked his interest: a bright yellow piece of plastic that was molded to resemble a human femur, or thigh bone. Rolling the toy up from the end into a tight ball caused a prolonged wail that continued as a loud whistle when released to sail through the air, diminishing as it unfurled. Sabre's ears perked up, and he summoned the energy to take off in his wobbling gait across the back yard to retrieve the newest attraction.

Nissa invented her own variation for this new game. As Sabre headed back to me with this noisy toy securely in his mouth, she would run at him as if she intended to snatch his plastic bone away. Turning his head with a move that would be the envy of an NFL player, he kept possession. Nissa barked as she darted past. Quite proud of himself, he would bring his prize back to me to roll and toss again. The new game seemed to give his energy level a boost and became a frequent form of entertainment that also provided exercise and fun.

The endeavor sometimes turned into a game of chase, Nissa running for safety under the holly hedge, with Sabre in pursuit. They ended their fun with kisses amidst the sounds of panting and a foray under the holly branches, which, coincidentally, provided a back scratch for each of them. Sabre had rescued Nissa from being a target for aggression. She then found a way to repay his kindness with an enterprise that brought laughter as well as physical benefit.

Those play sessions were necessarily brief, but the rewards extended throughout the evening. Following a brief rest, I began the rather extensive preparations for their supper. Sabre's bowl was filled with kibbles and water, a spoonful of pumpkin, and a long list of vitamin supplements, while Nissa got her own food plus a healthy portion of vitamins. Flavoring was an important ingredient, as well. Their favorite was chicken livers baked in the oven and parceled into the rather unattractive, at least by human standards, mixture. The resulting resonance of the dinner hour filled the kitchen. Their slurping and chomping sometimes rivaled the intensity of a boisterous waterfall, each of them gobbling away in ecstasy.

After dinner, dessert arrived in the form of an ice cube crunching party, one of Sabre's favorite perks. After I softened each ice cube in water, they lay side by side and enjoyed the icy treats by crushing the cubes with their powerful jaws, as I dripped water on their faces and chuckled while ice chips flew in every direction. They looked up, expectantly awaiting the next one that I placed between their paws or slipped into their mouths.

Those moments of apparent normality led to contemplation of the multitude of lessons that dogs have to teach us. Rather than being mired in the throes of sadness over what was or what was not to be, they lived in a world that focused on the pleasures they could touch or that touched them. Living with DM, despite its unavoidable destination, became a life of simple pleasures, each precious moment enjoyed without restraint.

Chapter 42
A Special Day

Little more than a year had gone by since his diagnosis of Degenerative Myelopathy. Sabre had slipped from a robust, happy, and healthy dog to one with a body that appeared to be that of two dogs. His chest and front legs were still massive though appropriately proportioned to the size of his body; his muscles were strong in front and able to hold his weight while working to pull his rear end along. His back legs had shrunk to the size of a dog half his size. But somehow, through it all, he was still happy. His eyes were bright, his affection for Nissa and for me never waned, and each day held the same excitement for him that had consistently epitomized my "go anywhere, do anything dog."

I was no longer able to schedule or plan walks, but remained aware of his fluctuating energy level. I tried to gauge the amount of coordination he displayed during the day. I knew he missed this favorite activity, and I compensated by taking him and Nissa for rides more often. The atrophy of muscles in his back legs prevented him from being able to hop into the truck unaided, but he still tried. Somehow, he managed to get his front feet planted on the edge of the floorboard, one slow step at a time.

Although at first he didn't want help, he learned to wait expectantly for me to cup his back legs in my arms and lift him up. I had to move quickly to assist him before his back legs gave way. We repeated the maneuver to get him onto the back seat. Once there, he was able to move about, lie down with his head above the bottom of the window where he could see out, or even to sit up on better days. The floor was stuffed with pillows so that braking or a sudden stop wouldn't toss him about. There was no space for him to fall.

Getting out required coordination between his desire to exit on his own and my being close enough to catch his back legs before they hit the ground and he collapsed, as I knew now that he would. The remaining trace of independence seemed to revive some of his lost abilities and he would stagger into the house on his own. The balance between the inordinate effort and his enjoyment of going for a ride meant having to constantly monitor his energy and mobility on a daily basis. Yet again, he accepted the changes with grace and a discernible touch of dignity, as he made his way through the house to his favorite place in the hall on the cool travertine floor.

Over the months, I spent as little time away from the house as possible, going to the grocery store on the way home from work and carefully planning my route to pick up the items I needed with efficiency and brevity. Visits on holidays were limited to the fewest possible hours away in order to get back home. I maximized my moments with him, the knowledge that I would not have him with me as long as I wanted constantly in my awareness. Letty had said that he only wanted to be with me, and I only wanted to be with him. Nissa seemed to share my sentiments. I noticed her lying at his side more than in the past.

Sabre was particularly perky one afternoon, so I took his leash and boots off the counter to prepare for a walk. His excitement, accompanied by an imitation of his happy dance, brought Nissa running to see what was going on. I thought I would have to hogtie both of them to get his boots on his feet. Nissa darted from side to side, lavishing kisses on my face and his and spinning around like a puppy. Sabre kept trying to get up, jerking his feet away just as I attempted to fasten the Velcro, and several times I had to start the process over. Finally, I somehow managed to get his boots secured and the leash through the loop of his collar.

He bounded out the door and down the sidewalk, pulling me behind him with a strength I couldn't believe was still there. On the circular driveway two doors away from the house, cats scattered in all directions shocked to see their nemesis barreling down on them with determination and drive. Sabre stopped, repeating his revised happy dance, and looked up at me proudly, as if to say, "Look what I just did!" He seemed so pleased with his accomplishment that I laughed out loud.

He wasn't finished. He pulled me along and headed for the next obvious place where he could wreak more havoc on the lounging feline population. Cats hissed, growled, and ran for safety with expressions of displeasure that rivaled his show of exuberance. Sabre was back and he was overjoyed! The cats were adamant that they did not share his enthusiasm. They stared out from behind bushes, under porches, and the tops of fences. Had they been able to summarize their collective sentiments into a single exclamation, my ears would have burned for days. I hadn't seen Sabre's happy dance in quite some time, but that day I was treated to the joyous sight on several occasions. His energy continued for close to a two block walk, the longest he'd been able to last in months. When we finally arrived home, I found that I was the one whose energy was depleted. Nissa, however, was not to be denied her opportunity to add to the fray.

I unhooked the leash and removed his boots. Sabre settled at the front windows to watch, and Nissa practically hurdled through the door, her excitement heightened by the wait for her turn. She was disappointed at having nothing to chase. Sabre's unexpected reign of terror had left them all in hiding, so Nissa had to be content with searching and sniffing. Not a single cat was in sight. Sabre had stolen her thunder.

Chapter 43
If Only You Could Talk

Our next excursion wasn't as exhilarating. Although Sabre started out strong, pulling against the leash and charging forward with his head held high, he soon began to falter. His back legs crossed, he lost his strength, and he twisted to the ground. After each fall, I helped him back up. He resisted my efforts to get him to turn toward home. He didn't want to quit.

I kept him in the grass as much as possible so he wouldn't fall on the concrete, but after passing only three houses, he needed to rest. I settled into the grass beside him as he placidly viewed the activity on the street. I was torn between crying and anger.

He didn't deserve what was happening to him. The calmness and serenity in his face made my rising fury seem somehow out of place. I wondered if he knew he was dying. Silently, in my mind only, I bargained for the words to tell him just how much he meant to me. I knew that he understood me without the benefit of words, but I said out loud the words most repeated by people who love dogs. "If only you could talk."

Slipping my arms around his neck, I buried my face in his soft, lush coat, not caring what anyone thought. Holding him close to me was all that mattered as the minutes slipped by, each one precious. Finally, I brushed away the remnants of tears on my face as he looked up, letting me know he was ready to try again.

Despite him wanting to continue, his strength had ebbed, and even his determined will couldn't overcome what he had lost. I bent at the waist, held his legs up, and walked slowly behind him back to the house. I'm sure we were quite the sight, like one of those two-people horses in comedy shows, but without the benefit of a costume. Sabre seemed to catch my thought and twisted back to plant a long wet kiss across my face. We both ended up on the ground in a tangle of fur and skin. Sabre felt no pain, finding a wonderfully captive audience for his affection. All I could do was laugh.

The brief respite provided just enough energy to reach the front door. I brought his bowl of water to him, ignoring for a moment Nissa's protests, as he settled in front of the windows. Not to be denied her place in the sun, Nissa jumped, twisted, and poked me with her nose until I grabbed her leash and took her out for her turn.

This time, the complacent cat population was waiting, nestled in cool hedges and stretched out on driveways. Nissa charged and they ran for their lives, hisses and growls lingering in the air after they had disappeared. Nissa was appeased, her hunt was successful, and we returned home for the long awaited dinner hour.

Chapter 44
A Place for Hedgehog

Each time I started thinking that the day for the dreaded decision was imminent, DM would grant a small reprieve. Sometimes his achievements were as simple as being able to go to the kitchen for water or come into the office to be beside me. However, every gain was short-lived, and he again lay down as if the effort had drained all his energy away.

Having watched Sabre try to get up from the floor, then twisting backwards when his legs would not hold his weight, I searched through the house to find Hedgehog. Maybe during the night or when I was occupied with something else, he had retrieved his favored companion from the living room. Hedgehog was at the windows in the kitchen. I fluffed the make-believe fur and presented his favorite toy. Grasping Hedgehog firmly in his mouth, the familiar look of gratitude spread across his face.

When I told him out loud that Hedgehog could go with him, a veil slipped over his expression, but I couldn't read the meaning. I was puzzled, feeling a little out of touch, and finding no clues in his eyes as to what he might be thinking. I returned to working on a design I had to deliver later.

After a few minutes, I heard his wobbly gait as he came into the office, Hedgehog clenched in his jaws. I started to smile at the familiar sight, and I swiveled my chair around to watch as he approached. Instead of lying down, he carefully placed Hedgehop beside me, and then turned to go back to the hall. As clearly as if he had spoken, I knew at that moment that he wanted Hedgehog to stay with me. Struggling to hold back my tears, I picked it and held it. When I was certain my voice would not betray the emotions welling up inside, I took Hedgehog back to him. Sitting on the floor beside him, stroking his head, I simply said, "For now, we'll share." He seemed to understand, and satisfied, laid his head between his paws.

As if he wanted to be certain he had communicated his wish, for the next couple of days, I'd hear his familiar ambling gait as he placed Hedgehog at my side. He reminded me of the day he stood behind Nissa, refusing to lie down, until he was certain she was coming home with us. Sabre had made his wishes known.

Chapter 45

Borrowed Courage

In the dark hours of the morning, dawn soaked only the edges of night from the sky, and both dogs were napping after their breakfast. I returned to the Internet discussion group. The typed messages had become my safety net when emotion threatened to tear away my self-control. Our communications formed a highway lined with kindred spirits who had endured what I was facing. I could always count on a response, usually several. Replies to the thoughts I expressed were kind, supportive, and void of judgment. Theirs was an understanding that only comes from having walked the path of loss and heartache.

Living with DM is akin to playing the old arcade game of waiting for prairie dogs to pop up from their holes and hitting them with a mallet. When one was struck, two or three more popped up in other places. Keeping up is nearly impossible. With DM, the game can never end or be won, but those facts stops no one from praying for the miracle that will not happen.

Even with the sympathy of friends and the empathy from members of the forum, I still felt like I was living on top of a shattered, fragmented mirror, the pieces lying at odd angles on the floor, waiting to slice the unsuspecting foot. The odd feeling crept in as if what was happening was somehow my fault. I couldn't divorce what lay ahead from my thoughts or my mental search for that thing I had done wrong. When I was away from the house and Sabre couldn't know, I allowed the tears to fall. I couldn't decide if the release was self-pity that spared him from the upsetting emotions, or early grief.

By contrast, Sabre's calm serenity was my borrowed courage, keeping me going when the weak human in me wanted to quit. As he looked directly in my eyes, I sensed that he was seeing something beyond my vision, and that he had wisdom that was out of my reach that only he could touch. When I stared into his eyes, his strength, in a manner I couldn't explain, became part of me. His gift was the opportunity every day to be better than I had been the day before, to go a little beyond what I thought I couldn't do. I learned to put aside the pain of impending loss to take each moment in front of me as a precious treasure.

Those intervals of contemplation were when I realized Sabre had always been my anchor. No matter how rough life seemed, he was there beside me, and I drew strength from him. He was my angel with a tail.

Maybe out of love, or maybe out of pure insanity, I started calling the answering machine when I had to be away from the house. Once when a friend was visiting, she'd told me that when I talked to the machine, Sabre and Nissa went to the office to listen. Somehow, I needed to keep my connection with Sabre unbroken and I'd found a way to keep Nissa firmly within the circle.

Along with regular calls to Ronnie, I kept Letty appraised of Sabre's condition. She had loaned a cart and a number of slings to help him as the DM progressed, but he had resisted each device, preferring to maneuver on his own. As long as he could get from place to place without hurting himself, I decided that letting him do what he wanted was best.

My concern reached devastating proportions on the afternoon he reached the middle of the back yard, trying to reach out to Nissa as she tried to engage him in a game of chase. As she swept past, he lost his balance, and his legs splayed, but he somehow managed to stay upright with his beautiful tail lifeless and dragging on the ground. He stayed in that position until he began to shake. His atrophied muscles threatened to dump him on the ground. I held off from going to him, waiting for a sign that he wanted my help. He stood for what seemed to be several minutes, looking from side to side, lost as to what to do next. His tentative attempts to adjust only resulted in a quick return to his previous stance, unable to move forward, reluctant to move back for fear of falling, desperately trying to maintain balance.

I stepped back into the house and grabbed one of the slings. When I started to put the bright red harness around his rear, he didn't resist. I pulled on the straps to elevate his back legs and he immediately responded. Too quickly for me to prepare, he took off across the yard in pursuit of Nissa. He chased her to the bushes and followed her across the yard, while I trailed along like someone whose coattail got stuck in the door as the car moved away and accelerated. The back yard suddenly seemed the size of a football field as Sabre and Nissa frolicked from corner to corner and back again. Fearing I'd have to call 911 if I continued, I finally got the two of them to calm down enough to go back in the house. I thought Sabre would surely need water, so I headed toward the kitchen.

He had other ideas. He forcefully bypassed the water bowl and headed for the front door to go for a walk. I couldn't help but laugh at his exuberance and the noise of loud panting, nails scraping the hard floors, and Nissa's puppy yips as we swarmed through the house like a captured tornado. I hadn't seen either of them as happy in several months. Undaunted by my refusals, he struck out for the garage door to go for a ride, pulling me along with a strength that had been absent for months.

I looked directly into Sabre's face and his sudden surge of activity made sense. Just like his tail that I had patiently bathed and dressed until it healed, just like his ears that I had cleaned and medicated until the terrible itch went away and his hair grew back, just like every nick and scrape he'd had, he thought the DM had gone away. His expression delivered an unmistakable message: he knew if he remained patient long enough, I'd make this right, too. Sabre thought, "I'm fixed!"

His joy, fanned through the aid of the sling, made his eyes dance with ecstasy, but when I reluctantly removed the sling and his back legs sagged to the floor, I watched the spark in his eyes dim. The crushing heartache of DM, an engulfing invisible vortex of cruel destruction, declared an irrevocable triumph in that single moment of perfect desolation.

Sabre's independence was the mark of his existence, the symbolic freedom from his earlier life of restraint. From the moment he was given his head to go where he pleased, he had insisted on doing things for himself. Even when he was lifted from the floor to the vet's examination table, he tried to help. Legs reaching and paws scrabbling at the edge of the table repeatedly made the task more difficult than if he had remained passive. When the disease caused difficulty bounding into the truck, he refused to wait for my help.

The recognition in his eyes was as clear as if he'd spoken. He realized he would never again run free or frolic at will. Silent tears overcame me and my breath came in ragged spurts, as I watched his spirit sink behind the dark, cavernous recesses of his eyes, becoming barren of hope in an instant. He had coped with every change the insidious disease had thrown at him, but that loss eroded the core of his being.

There would be no going back to hopping into the truck to find adventure in the next destination, no more carefree walks, cavorting down the sidewalks, and no more chasing cats and sniffing trees. In the suffocating pain of losing before the battle was lost, Sabre, Nissa, and I were fixed in place, paralleling the frozen frame of a movie stuck in the projector, edges starting to burn as flames danced across the screen. We had been struck down by the reality we'd tried to outrun.

Chapter 47
Reaching Beyond

There were no tricks left to play. I'd run out of chips to bargain with for more time. There were no more exercise programs to devise, no more seeking new nutrients to add to his food, no more hope of stimulating nerves that could not respond. The only thing left to observe was Sabre, even though his vibrant spirit that lived within those deep brown eyes and filled with joy whenever I looked in his direction was fading.

In a desperate effort to revive our success with the sling from the day before, I put the sling on Sabre the next morning to go outside. He showed little interest, merely tolerating the maneuvers necessary to help him along. When we went back in the house, he managed to reach his place in the hall, where he quietly settled against the wall. Even Nissa's ferocious growls at the cats passing in front of her windows provided no distraction from his vacant stare. Yet, when he saw me looking in his direction, the expression of devotion was still as clear as if we were headed out the door for some new and exciting adventure.

Linda, one of the moderators of my Internet discussion group, and others encouraged observing a dog with DM when he didn't know he was being watched. "You will find," they all said, "in that one moment, the answer to the question of how long."

I feared that Sabre's sharp ears would detect sounds of my movement, but a few minutes later, as quietly as I could, I went to my office door. The sadness in his eyes and his empty stare cut through my heart and left a ruthless, brutal wound. I struggled to breathe in a void that formed the emotional equivalent of an exploding grenade that forced air from a room. The look on his face told me his last defeat had irreparably damaged his indomitable spirit, the courage that he had always shown throughout the sinister progression of DM. He was still my "Sabre dog," but his life had become an abyss that spoiled his joy. He found no more reasons to fight, and the loss couldn't come back.

I could not imagine a world without Sabre at my side, but I returned to my computer and read the section I had avoided, the one entitled "Making the Final Decision."

Tears rolled from my eyes as I searched within for a courage I didn't possess, a strength I didn't own, grappling with the knowledge that I had to do the thing I could not do. No matter the pain I felt, I had a promise to keep. My vow to Sabre was that I would not keep him with me at the price of him being miserable. I had read enough about the disease to know that physically, the dangers of keeping his body alive through the inevitable disintegration from within would lead to damage of his organs, neural distortion, and, worst of all, seizures.

I had spared him the insults along the way. Had he known that elimination had become a part of his walks, I'm sure he would have been mortified. I never allowed him to know, returning to pick up the sidewalks as Nissa and I followed in his tracks.

He had been spared other indignities. I wouldn't allow him to feel discomfort from oversensitivity to heat or dehydration that could have occurred. I wouldn't allow him to lose his ability to breathe, or to soil himself in the natural functions of living. Sabre had lived his life gracefully, with dignity and gratitude. He deserved the considerations I felt certain he would choose for himself.

As if to punctuate the decision I now knew was imminent, that night when I put his food bowl in front of him, he turned away, refusing to eat. There was no mistaking his message. He had never turned away from food or from me before.

The next night, he again refused his food, and only ate when I placed handfuls of his dinner in front of his mouth. He ate to please me, but I couldn't ignore the wish that he could not express in any other way.

As I sat on the floor feeding him each bite, a phrase came to mind that I hadn't thought of in decades. "For those to whom much is given, much more is required." I had never known its true meaning until that moment.

The well-known cartoon light bulb came on in my brain as I realized the importance of those words. Sabre was the gift I knew I did not deserve and had not earned. He was loving and forgiving, but I was selfish, seizing for myself what I claimed because I could. He gave with every part of his heart and soul. What I had given at times had been grudging before the devastation to his body and the impending loss of his companionship had forced me to reach beyond myself.

As these thoughts cascaded through my awareness, he looked up from the floor. I knew, without the benefit of words, through the brief glimmer of light in his eyes, that I had been granted a rite of passage surpassing the human condition, the ability to give without the expectation of return. The ultimate price was saying goodbye to a soul that had become part of my being. Yet somehow, in that same moment, he imparted the belief that his gift would remain behind. His courage and strength would forever be a part of me as unforgettable as the essence of love that characterized his life.

I called Ronnie the next morning, describing in objective terms the physical phenomena I saw in Sabre. The quiet on the other end of the phone as Ronnie listened drowned out the false courage I'd mustered to make the call. My words trailed off into silence, catching in my throat, restraining my ability to speak.

I couldn't say the thoughts that tried to form in my mind; they were trapped between knowing my time with Sabre was at the end, and wanting with every part of my being to hold on to him forever.

Ronnie gave me a moment to grasp what I already knew. His voice was gentle and compassionate. "It sounds like he's reached the point where his suffering is more than he can handle."

"I know," I managed to say. "I know what I'm seeing in his eyes. I know what he's telling me. He can't do it any more; it's just too much for him."

Hot tears welled up in my eyes, rolling down my face, silent sobs escaping as I sank to the ground. DM would grant no more reprieves. The moment I dreaded had finally arrived. I felt I was being ripped slowly apart, like fabric weakened by the weather, each strand breaking, one by one. I'd never known a pain so deep, a pain that instinctively I knew would never completely go away.

"Are you going to be okay?"

"Yes," was all I could manage, but I didn't believe my own words.

Ronnie waited a few seconds more. "Let me go look at my schedule."

My call had come in on the private number in his office

where he keeps his schedule on his desk. The silence on the other end of the line betrayed no sound of movement. "I don't want to make him have to wait any longer than is necessary, but it looks like the first day I can get over there is Thursday. Is that going to be alright?"

I took a deep breath, letting it out slowly. All I could say was, "Thank you."

I watched rays of light streaming through the gaps in the trees into the office windows as they gave way to a foggy barrier that turned the July heat into a barren world with no warmth.

I shivered as I retreated to the back yard, leaving both dogs behind me. I sat on the ground and cried. For several minutes, I stood there with my hands helplessly at my side. Pain distorted my face like a six-year-old whose ice cream cone has fallen to the hot pavement and was rapidly melting beyond retrieval. I had to remind myself to breathe.

Finally, the flurry of emotion started to calm, my trembling halted, and I opened my eyes. I reminded myself that Sabre deserved only my best effort, no less than he had given me. I resolved to find the way to say goodbye. Slowly, a plan began to form in my mind.

I erased the signs of crying from my face, and then I went back inside to put the plan into motion. I took a couple of steaks out of the freezer for a dinner for three I planned to cook. The remaining days would be a celebration of Sabre's life.

Sitting close to him on the floor with his brushes arrayed around his quiet form, I gently pulled them through his thick, luxurious coat. I sensed his understanding that I knew what he wanted. As if in relief, he stretched and uttered a happy snort of pleasure.

Although the muscles of my mouth quivered, my voice was surprisingly calm and modulated when I told him the story of The Rainbow Bridge. "Sabre, there's an old Norse legend that describes a lush meadow with fragrant flowers and sunlight with trees for shade, a place of peace and contentment, where all the pets separated from their people wait. In the swaying grass, old ones were made young, those whose bodies had suffered injury or been ravaged by disease were made whole. Together, those friends frolic and play, never tire, and wait for the reunion with the people they love."

Sabre closed his eyes and settled back to enjoy being groomed. I told him, "I'll meet you there and we'll cross over that bridge under the rainbow. We'll be together again forever."

He opened his eyes as I finished the story. Peace saturated the dark brown eyes that I loved. Intending to lessen his fears, I had inadvertently lessened my own. Nissa, managing to escape my notice, had slipped in and was lying quietly on the floor beside us. I reached over and scratched her ear, patted Sabre on the head, and then got up to prepare for the next event in our celebration of Sabre's life.

Chapter 49

Celebration

Ever cautious of his waning energy, I timed the activities in between periods of rest. I wanted him to enjoy every moment earmarked for him. After grooming, we went for a ride. Even on a weekday, I knew people would be walking their dogs.

Nissa was glad to go along for moral support, and leaped into the truck with her usual gusto. Although Sabre reached the truck on his own, I had to support him with my knees, pulling his front legs up first, followed by lifting his back legs from the garage floor, repeating the process from the floorboard to the seat. He tried to help and I encouraged him, his look of gratitude present on his face as he made himself comfortable.

As I'd hoped, the trails held a reasonable number of walkers and their canine companions. Sabre watched with intent interest, and I slowed the truck, waving and smiling as we passed. He was clearly enjoying the outing, resting briefly, then sitting up again so he would not miss the sights. Nissa practiced rare restraint, staying to her side of the seat, even when there was nothing to see. I knew she loved him as much as I did, and she showed her affection with wet slurpy kisses on his cheek. However, this was not to be the end of our excursion. I had another surprise in mind.

We left the park, but instead of turning right to go back home, I turned in the opposite direction, continuing down the avenue. Several blocks later, left signal blinking as I waited to cross traffic, both dogs' ears perked up as they sniffed the wonderful aromas pouring into the back window from Sonic. They could barely contain their excitement as I pulled in and leaned out to place the order. Our infrequent visits there had usually produced the predictable result of me getting to eat only half of my French fries and most of my corn dog, but only if I had smeared it with mustard first. This time, the treat was theirs.

I listened to their muffled whines of excitement and doled out the fries as fast as they chomped, jaws closing down, lips smacking. Nissa dived to the floorboard after any tiny morsel that dropped. This time, Sabre shared his own corn dog with Nissa. The look on Nissa's face said he didn't quite divide this delicacy equally, but she was still a happy little girl. A glance at Sabre's expression revealed a contentment that had been absent for quite awhile.

When we returned home, I started to help Sabre over to his favorite place in the hall, but he evaded my efforts, apparently determined to get there on his own. Standing back, I watched his muscles quiver with the effort. He had invented yet another way to cope; leaning against the wall to absorb his weight, he settled smoothly to the floor. His look of gratitude emphasized the importance that being independent held for him, a trait we shared.

I called Nissa over to us, belly rubs being the next order of business. My arms eventually tired, but there was no impulse to get up, to leave the tiny refuge of serenity we'd created Sabre rested, napping peacefully with his eyes closed as he restored his energy.

I feared that DM would steal our laughter away, but we had laughed with abandon throughout the day at Nissa diving for French fries and Sabre trying to capture the errant sliver of crust from the corn dog that landed on his nose, his tongue flicking at it until it somehow landed in his mouth. My eyes traced the once powerful muscles in his back legs that had shriveled into a parody of what he had once been to the strength that was still present in his face. I had learned a new language from Sabre, the language of courage.

From watching him with Nissa or simply being with him, I learned to listen to the "quiet" and to read his moods. He taught me that a minute, an hour, a day, or a week is simply a moment, and that all moments can become treasured gifts destined not to fade away, but to live forever in the heart. He had shown me that we didn't need to talk in order to be heard, and that a touch can mean more than words. He taught me that trying to make rational what is ultimately irrational is an exercise in futility that only drains the heart and soul. He taught me to live and to love, and that nothing is more important.

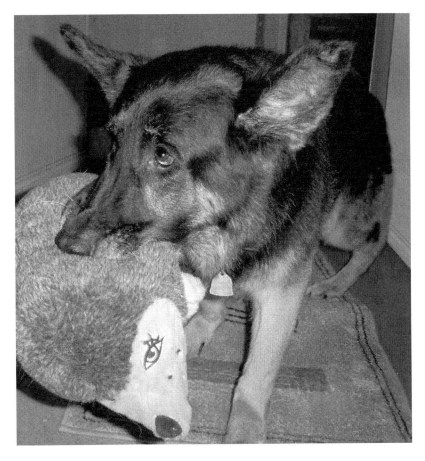

Sabre on his last day. He made a courageous effort to carry Hedgehog through the house as he'd always done, coping with his instability by leaning against the walls to be able to walk. Courtesy of Marty Mann.

Chapter 50

Ice Cube Party

The festivities continued. Aside from Nissa's pronounced dislike for being brushed, I kept Nissa involved in all aspects.

In the kitchen, I filled a large plastic glass with ice, adding water to soften the cubes. Nissa observed to make sure I got the recipe correct.

I was surprised when Sabre made his way to the couch unassisted, anticipation sparkling across his features. They lay at my feet, happily chomping their way through the ice cubes offered for their enjoyment. Then, they were treated to another glass, and then to another. Ice chips flew in every direction. They attached to the sides of their mouth, lodged on the tops of their noses, and landed as far away as a few feet from where they smacked their lips with obvious pleasure. They consumed four full glasses!

The party ended when one errant chip found lodged in Nissa's ear. She didn't know whether to spit, sneeze, roll, or run away. She bounced to her feet, shaking her head furiously. The look on her face was one of shock and dismay packaged with an indignant snort worthy of a queen. She stood stiffly as if to emphasize her opinion of this indignity. Sabre watched with his mouth open, and I started laughing. Nissa was apparently offended at my bad behavior, and with an even haughtier snort, stalked off to the front windows, pointedly ignoring us both.

I knew what I had to do. I placed the glass on the table, patted Sabre, and went to the front room. Nissa refused to acknowledge me until I had appropriately rendered the required apologies, reassurance that she was still the most beautiful and noble Lady German Shepherd in the city, and an ample amount of groveling pleas for her return to the circle. Satisfied, she came back to the living room. I had to suppress my chuckles or risk a repeat of her pronounced exit.

Sabre, by that time, had discounted Nissa's outburst and cheerfully cleaned up from the carpet all the chips of ice left behind. He graciously enjoyed all the mechanisms of our celebration of his life, looking out through his dark eyes with the love that powered his existence. I was again awed by his presence, the gentle strength exuding from the wise spirit within. I was reminded of one of my favorite Gibran quotes: "Keep me from the wisdom which does not cry, the philosophy which does not laugh, and the greatness which does not bow before children . . . ." In my mind, I added, ". . . and dogs."

Sabre's last ice cube crunching party. His back legs had become a shadow of what they once were.

Chapter 51

Cheerios and Vanilla Wafers

The next day, I struggled with the thought that my last day with him had come. Sabre seemed to have moved past the anxiety and quiet desperation of the nights before when he refused to eat. He was calm, although a sense of tiredness remained just under the surface. I sensed a weariness unrelated to physical strength that ran deeper than a simple need for rest. I found I didn't need to pretend exuberance or paint the minutes with the lighthearted demeanor that characterized the day before.

Silent recognition of the reality before us transformed the inherent sadness into a solid knowledge that the path before us was the right one for Sabre. The magnificent love he'd given would be returned to him in granting his desire for release from what his physical life had become. His three wishes, to have a home, to own a human, and to have Nissa as his companion, transcended to his fourth and final wish: to be freed from the ravages of DM.

Instead of pouring a first cup of coffee and ambling to the computer, I brought my coffee to a place on the floor beside him and sat with my arm around his neck. As if I had read his mind, rather than him always reading mine, he looked up with his unyielding gaze of gratitude and love.

We sat there together in the quiet of the morning, his head in my lap and his heart in my hands. Solace came through thoughts of his freedom returned. Comfort came from visions of the meadow at the rainbow bridge where he would once again be whole, frolicking through the grass with the others. The hint of unrest receded. Although the pain of impending loss danced in shadows around my heart, nothing could overshadow my sense of gratitude that I'd been granted the privilege of having had him at all. Sabre was my dream dog, and few have the good fortune of a dream come true.

Breakfast, in addition to the never to be missed Milk-Bone upon rising, was enhanced by a curious mixture of Cheerios and vanilla wafers, two of Sabre's favorites. I put an ample amount in his bowl and, likely to Nissa's dismay, a respectable but lesser portion in hers. She was not to be fooled, looking up as she finished, as if to say, "Is that all I get?" I chuckled as she hovered close to Sabre, hoping, maybe, he wouldn't want all of his. As I stood by and watched, he moved away from his dish leaving a sizable bite for his puppy to enjoy.

Sabre on July 9, 2009, waiting for Ronnie. Courtesy of Marty Mann.

Letty's words, "he only wants to be with you," fluttered through my thoughts all morning and through the rest of the day. Except for the steak dinner I would cook later for him, simply being together became the plan of the day. I put on a favorite CD by Shastro, "Visions of Shambala." I'd noticed on other occasions that he seemed drawn to that particular music, often leaving the coolness of the hall floor to lie beside my chair in the office as the melodies floated through the room. This time I used the larger speakers in the living room and, placing Hedgehog between his paws, watched as his eyes played across various places in the house as if he was memorizing the sights.

Barely aware of the time passing, reluctant to disturb the peaceful togetherness, I got up from the floor to cook his steak. As I went through the preparations, Sabre dragged himself across the rug to the kitchen door to be close enough to see what was happening.

Nissa was astutely aware that the hour wasn't typical for dinner. She danced around with anticipation equal to a performance of circus clowns, getting underfoot and leaning against my leg in just the direction I needed to go next. Her boldness was a tribute to Sabre's compassionate mentoring of the pup whose shyness once kept her in the background, striving hard to do the right things, never make mistakes, or get in the way. She bounced around with an abandon that only a healthy confidence in herself could endow, the essential embodiment of joy for a happy little girl.

At last, dinner was served. The meal was heaven on earth! Sabre and Nissa gobbled their way through the bite-sized presentation that was cooked to perfection.

After I cleaned up their bowls and took Sabre's water over to him, I retrieved his brushes, grooming him before the arrival of our two best friends, Marty and Gloria, whom Sabre loved as much as I did. As they walked through the door, I caught Sabre's glances as he searched in anticipation of Holly and Candy. Seeing the door close without his beautiful Poodle cousins following, he seemed to understand and devoted his attention to the party at hand. He was delighted they'd come to visit him. Feebly, but determined, he bought Hedgehog to the kitchen, placing his favored toy beside Gloria, as he settled in between his honored guests.

About an hour passed in soft conversation before Ronnie's truck pulled up in front of the house. Sabre's ears perked up and Nissa ran to the windows. Surprisingly, neither barked as Ronnie approached the door. With an unexpected burst of energy, Sabre got to his feet, slowly made his way over to Ronnie, and kissed his hands. Small whimpers from Nissa escaped into the room, barely audible along with our spoken greetings. Ronnie reached down and ruffled his fur, while Nissa competed for his attention. I placed a cup of coffee in front of his chair and filled the other cups.

Ronnie was in no hurry. He settled comfortably into the discussion, while I slipped away to sit beside Sabre on the floor. I was soon lost to the interaction taking place, holding Sabre close, running my hands through his fur, softly whispering in his ears. His contentment was obvious. He lay quietly without stirring.

Chapter 52

A Little Help from My Friends

My silent reverie was broken when Ronnie softly said he'd like to give Sabre a shot to be sure he remained relaxed so that nothing would frighten him. I couldn't believe that Sabre would ever be afraid of anything, but Ronnie wanted to be certain. Sabre's trust in him was total, as was mine, and I nodded in agreement.

Sabre's eyes opened briefly as Ronnie knelt beside him, talking to him as he'd always done and petting his head, as I held his leg up for Ronnie to find the vein. As the liquid flowed in, he closed his eyes again with a soft sigh. Sabre seemed to know that his misery was soon to end.

As we sat there on the floor, speaking in hushed tones, my eyes stayed remarkably dry. The pain of parting was held at bay. The courage I'd gained from Sabre overruled my frail, human emotions.

Ronnie surveyed his quiet form, his barely discernible breathing, and finally said, "You know, except for the DM, this dog is in perfect physical condition. He doesn't even look his age."

Sabre drifted deeper into the induced slumber. Ronnie looked over at me. I knew he was telling me that the time had come.

I could only nod in agreement, unable to trust my voice.

He gently slipped the new syringe into the plastic end of the needle and slowly administered the drug that would stop Sabre's heart. He reached for his stethoscope several times to listen for his heartbeat, only to put it aside to wait again. After the third or fourth time, he looked down at Sabre and gently said, "He's gone."

At once tears exploded from my eyes and seared my face.

Breathing came in gasps. My eyes closed tight, as I buried my face in his coat as if that could somehow stop all the pent up emotions surging to the surface.

Sensing my need for solitude in my last moments with Sabre, Ronnie returned to his seat. After a few moments of silence, the hushed conversation of my friends resumed, yielding a delicate curtain of privacy for me to say goodbye. Nissa wandered over, studying him and sniffing his head and ears. Then, she walked quietly to her corner where she lay down with her head between her paws.

No one indicated a need to get up or move away. I stayed on the floor beside Sabre, holding him close to me, clinging to the soul I knew was no longer there. We remained entwined in a final loving embrace until my thoughts came back around.

The better part of an hour had passed until my consciousness reacquainted with my surroundings. I arose to take Nissa outside to the back. For reasons I hardly understood, I didn't want her to see her Sabre taken out the front door.

Even in death, my responsibility to Sabre didn't end. I helped Ronnie take him out to the truck, and whispered as Ronnie stood back, "Goodbye, my Sabre dog."

As the truck pulled away, I stood watching until Ronnie drove out of sight.

Chapter 53

A Walk on Familiar Paths

Marty and Gloria stayed for a few minutes more, sensing my inability to respond in further conversation. There was nothing that could be said at the time, so they gathered up their things to leave.

I told them, "I'm grateful you were with me."

We walked to their car, retracing the sad steps I had taken only minutes before.

Nissa looked up as I came back into the house. I went to her, searching her eyes, knowing the importance of connecting with her. I knelt and hugged her in the quiet stillness. The house had never seemed emptier. Although I wanted more than anything to sink to the floor, Nissa needed reassurance.

I went to the closet, took her leash from the wall, and snapped the clip in the loop on her collar. Instead of her usual excited dance, she stood quietly, her soft brown eyes watching me. I led her to the door.

"Lets go, girl!"

As we started down the sidewalk, her pace slowly gained momentum. She gave chase to the lounging cats in the circular driveways, stopping to sniff where they'd been. Simply being in motion seemed to help dissipate the barren sense of desolation that had fallen on us inside the house. Although another hot Texas day had left the air thick without any discernible breeze, the sound of footsteps on the concrete was somehow reassuring, but I knew the sights and sounds would never again be exactly the same.

Ann, a neighbor we'd chatted with occasionally at the corner, was out in her yard. Her dogs charged the fence, vying to remain in front of each other as they barked, jumped, and fussed. Nissa was glued to the pickets, head down low to match their height, her rear end in the air, tail wagging furiously.

Ann came over to the fence. "How's your boy doing?"

When I tried to speak, the words caught in my throat, and the muscles in my face constricted into a grimace of pain. My eyes pleaded for explanations I couldn't form. "I just lost him about an hour ago." I didn't know the voice that emerged. The sounds were not mine. A stranger had spoken.

My eyes closed to shut out the fading light of the day, and my head slowly lowered toward the sidewalk. Ann remained quiet.

Drawing a ragged breath, I tried again, "It just got to be more than he could handle. It was too much for him to endure."

"I know it hurts, but you did the best thing for him."

I felt raw and numb at once. I could only manage a nod.

"We can talk later if you want; all you have to do is call if I can help."

"Thank you." Again, I heard a voice I didn't know.

Nissa and I continued around the block and returned home. After feeding her, I wandered through the house, unable to remain in any one place for very long. I left my book unopened, the TV off, and the computer dark, and I stared out the front windows without seeing.

I stopped to pet Nissa when she tired of trying to follow me. I looked over at the corner and saw Hedgehog on the floor. Taking Sabre's collar from the kitchen table, I slipped it around Hedgehog's neck. Cradling the proxy German Shepherd puppy in my arms, I carried him to my bedroom and gently placed him atop the armoire, gathering baby, Gabby Gorilla, Henrietta, and Jake the duck for company. Nissa trailed behind to observe, then went over to the bed, snuggling down in the first place she'd slept when she had come to stay. There was nothing left for this day but to go to sleep.

Nissa, sad and forlorn, missing Sabre.

Chapter 54

It's Not How Long the Flower Blooms

The next day when I went out to check the mail, I was surprised to see a bouquet of flowers on the porch with a card tucked among the brilliant red blossoms. The card from Ann read, "It's not how long the flower blooms, but how beautifully."

Flowers and plants began to appear on the steps as the next few days went by and word traveled through the neighborhood. I had only told Ann and Marsue, but I discovered cards stuck in the door, tucked under the mat, and slipped into the mailbox from people whose names I didn't recognize. I realized how deeply Sabre had touched those he'd met with his courage and his refusal to bow down when the fight was not his to win. I knew he had belonged to everyone, not just to me.

A couple of days later, I woke up from a dream. Dawn peaked through the windows, setting the room aglow. I rarely remember dreams when I awaken, but on that Sunday morning when I opened my eyes, I saw Sabre's face at the side of my bed, happy and young again! In the voice of a youngster away at summer camp, his enthusiasm brimming over, he spoke to me with excitement.

"I've met all the dogs from the list! Jack Flash the German Shepherd, Jake the Labrador Retriever, Jack the Corgi, Osten the Collie, Hobie the Boxer, Ragnar the German Shepherd, Spanky Lou the Sheltie, Denali the Great Pyrenees, Chance, Strasse, Zeus, and Rex! All the dogs who got to the meadow before me! They're all here. They welcomed me! The meadow at the Rainbow Bridge is full of soft grass, the flowers smell sweet, and all my favorite treats hang off the trees, even corn dogs and French fries! I can eat any time I want to. The river under the bridge is cool. We can drink it and then swim in it. It's not like our last days on Earth, we're whole again. We can run and play and we never get tired! I miss you, but I'm okay. And you will be, too. Don't cry . . . we'll be together again." As his happy face shimmered and faded away, he said, "And I can see colors!"

I woke, and though tears streamed down my face, I found that I was smiling because his spirit was firmly within my heart. Although gone from my side, I knew then he would always be with me.

Nissa was sitting by the bed as the images slowly faded from the shimmering brilliance that had dwarfed the rays of early dawn. The glow that painted the room had settled on her face and in her eyes.

Chapter 55
Brokaw, Gentleman Caller

I continued the walks with Nissa, taking her with me for short jaunts in the truck and visits to friend's houses. For the first few days, when we walked back in the door, she'd run from room to room, certain Sabre had probably gone to the groomer and would be there waiting for her. I missed him, too.

A shadow in the hall became Sabre lying in his favorite place. A tiny breeze was his soft muzzle playing across the top of my arm. I felt his absence. I longed for the sight of him waiting in the middle of the floor just outside of my shower. He chose the place, I'm sure, because that was when human beings smelled the best. A subtle realization, playing at the back of my mind crept slowly into prominence without rhyme or reason to the thought. When I believed it was me taking care of him, it had really been him pulling me through it all.

Nissa started hovering just outside the bedroom each morning until she'd hear me start to stir. Then, she charged through the door, a German Shepherd on a mission. With her trademark quick kiss, she turned and headed for the kitchen for her treat. Nissa, the puppy Sabre picked, was taking over the chore of waking her human. I had to smile.

Several weeks had passed when I got a call from Letty. She asked if I'd be home Saturday afternoon, saying that she and John would be driving up to Dallas and would like to come by. I welcomed the chance to visit, making a special trip on the day before to the grocery store for cheese, crackers, and other snacks. Letty would always be a treasured guest. Without her, I would have never had the privilege of my life with Sabre.

I answered the doorbell to Letty and John standing there with a gangly German Shepherd dog they introduced as Brokaw. Nissa thrust her head between the opened door and my leg, threatening to dislocate my knee and hopping like a rabid bunny rabbit as they made their way inside.

She proceeded to examine Brokaw from his airplane ears to his helicopter tail. Once he passed her inspection . . . playtime! Coquettishly curtsying in front of him, she invited him to join her for a romp. 200 pounds of German Shepherds playing is not particularly advisable in small places if you value the furniture, so we moved the party outside.

Nissa was delighted with this youngster, but Brokaw was smitten. He followed as she darted from corner to corner, trotting behind, bumping into her when she stopped suddenly. Then, both of them faced each other, danced on their hind legs, and dropped back to the ground nose to nose to start the chase again. Nissa's happiness was apparent, and my heart warmed to the sight of the most enthusiasm she'd shown in weeks.

Nissa's world held even more promise when Brokaw was invited for dinner, an invitation graciously accepted on his part. Soon, the time came for Letty and John to leave. While Brokaw was exploring with Nissa, they slipped out the door, waving goodbye. I waited until their van drove slowly away. Brokaw was not really aware at first that he'd been left behind, until he searched through the house and couldn't find them. With a stricken look on his face, he raced to the front window to look outside. Not quite sure of what he should do, he sat down, a lone sentinel scouring the street for a blue van.

Nissa and I tried to coax him away, but he was firmly dedicated to his task. An hour passed, then two hours, and still he sat gazing through the glass. Leaving him to his self-appointed task, I went into the living room and switched on the TV to catch the news.

Brokaw sat, dedicated to his vigil, certain that Letty and John would discover their mistake and come back for him. The darkness of the evening had reduced his view of the street to only small patches of ground at the base of the light poles. Nissa finally gave up her attempts to gain his attention and joined me in the other room.

In the shattered throes of dejection, Brokaw skulked into the hall, threw his head back, and howled. His decibel level and sheer desolation brought me straight up from my chair. Nissa leaped to her feet like a deer frightened from her lair. We ran to the hall, smothering the brokenhearted Brokaw in our embraces, and lavished affection and reassurance to sooth his poor deserted soul. He was sure they'd forgotten him and that he'd been abandoned and left in a strange place. He didn't know what to do.

After a couple of treats, an introduction to some of Sabre's old toys, and a look around that revealed even more toys, he started to change his mind. Nissa stayed at his side as he began to explore his surroundings with renewed interest, and then apparently decided that he didn't need any more of her help. He ambled off to lie down.

I watched in fascination as he got up to pace from the front of the house to the back, gathering toys and dropping them in a pile in the middle of the hall. I supposed he reasoned that if they did come back, he could at least take the toys with him as payment for all his suffering. He went about happily pursuing his task.

But if Brokaw thought the worst was over, his fears had just begun. Running out of toys to stack up, he ventured into my bedroom. For the first moments, all was quiet and no sounds of movement could be detected even though Nissa's ears were pitched sharply in the direction of the door.

We heard a low growl that graduated to a flurry of barking as Brokaw backed away from unimaginable dangers in that room, hackles on end, tail held stiffly, and his lip curled in furious determination.

I was immediately concerned that maybe one of the neighborhood opossums had found a way into the house. I grabbed up my heavy flashlight for protection, as I cautiously entered and turned on the lights, but I saw nothing there. I checked the closets, but again found nothing out of place.

Brokaw remained in the living room, not daring to venture

again into that palace of horrors. I looked at Nissa, but her attitude was that there was nothing to worry about, the same as mine.

Brokaw timidly peeked around the door frame, and I called him over, which seemed to pacify him as long as Nissa and I were with him. I couldn't figure out the dilemma until he took one tentative step toward the vanity. He peaked around the corner, his barking punctuated with intermittent squeaks, and he again ran from the room. My confused cleared when stood up and walked toward the opening. In the half light of the bedroom, I realized he had seen his own reflection in the mirrors. In his mind, there were German Shepherds trapped in the walls. He was outnumbered and he knew they'd get him if they ever escaped.

I laughed until my knees began to wobble and I finally collapsed to the floor. Nissa and I rolled around until Brokaw could stand it no longer. Keeping a wary eye on the dogs in the mirrors, he joined us on the floor. We played until Brokaw forgot his imminent danger, although his trips to the bedroom were marked with a prudent touch of caution for the next few days.

Nissa and Brokaw, So Happy Together.

Chapter 56
Forever Remembered, Forever Changed

I wish I could say that my grief soon receded, but my sorrow stayed in my innermost thoughts, even as I laughed at the joint antics of Nissa and Brokaw. If I accidentally dropped and broke a glass on the unforgiving travertine tiles, I broke into tears as if I'd destroyed a priceless piece of art. Tears came in the middle of laughter, unbidden, welling up from the sense of loss that I felt powerless to control or escape.

I drifted away from conversations, thoughts of Sabre more compelling than the exchange of ideas or interaction. Everything around me slowed down to a pace that rivaled being absorbed into a strange movie played out in slow motion. I fought with the demons of self blame, when the unwanted thoughts threatened to overrule the reality that there was nothing I could have done except for the things I did.

Even if I had known the answers to the questions floundering in the wake of Sabre's death, there was no magic solution for handling bereavement. There was no balm for my soul. Nothing soothed the pain or took away the smoldering anger. There was no halt to the lingering emptiness and sorrow.

Losing was a hollow, ragged feeling that burrowed deep inside, called up in an instant by a hint of coolness in heated air, a familiar fragrance, the wispy echo of a special song, or a word that speared my consciousness and couldn't be reined back in.

Whether for a person or a pet, loss leaves a hole in the heart that cannot be filled, that can only become obscured as time and distance wrap around the jagged edges.

Despite those residual emotions, Sabre had imparted yet another lesson: grief is individual and the visual traces don't give don't give license to judge the reason or the person.

Grief is personal, a symbol beyond the understanding of anyone who stands on the outside looking in. Mourning only proves that the reason behind its presence was a gift that shined more brightly than all others worthy of remembrance.

I was always so proud of my Sabre! He was beautiful, he was gentle, he was loving and affectionate, and often wise beyond the human realm. He departed with dignity, embraced by those who loved him, fifteen months from the time he was diagnosed until his legs gave out and the look in his eyes begged, "Help me . . . I can't do this anymore."

Our love for our furry friends knows no pride, no holding back, no lack of energy to do the things that must be done. In return, they give us their trust, their lives, their entire being. Their joy becomes our own, buying back for us our childhood sense of wonder that is so often lost in the process of growing older.

Letting go is painful, but not letting go when that's what they need most from us would be the ultimate betrayal. When the need arises for us to spare them further pain, our obligation is to provide release with the knowledge that our act of mercy is uncolored by selfishness. There is no distinction between physical, mental, or emotional pain. A gift equal to the love they bestow is required when life has become intolerable for them or when we know that worse dangers await around the next corner.

I knew when I brought him home with me that I wouldn't have him forever, but my life was enriched beyond all expectation by Sabre's wonderful spirit. I stayed on the discussion list to help others through their journey on the difficult path we had traveled, one that was made less lonely by the compassion of many dedicated people.

When we can find no words for ourselves, we rely on the messages of others to help us through the difficulties and doubts. Expression of our thoughts and feelings serve to soften the path of others. My connection to those kind souls will remain as an indelible part of my life. Luciano de Crescenzo wrote: "We are each of us angels with only one wing and we can only fly by embracing one another."

Sometimes as I watch the dawn creep across the sky, I still see Sabre bounding across the back yard with Nissa or wandering through the house with Hedgehog or Henrietta the Chicken in his mouth, still looking for that perfect place. I remember him quietly at my side, not caring what I was doing, satisfied to be with me. I cherish the memories of funny things he did that surprised and delighted me. I still can hear his grunts and snorts when I rubbed his belly. I laugh softly at the image of his impatience if I didn't get out of bed quite fast enough. Despite the pain in my heart and the tears that still come out of nowhere, I smile.

Sabre was dependent on me for food, shelter, and affection. I was dependent on him for compassion and humanity.

Nissa became the "big sister." Brokaw became the happy clown with his unprecedented ability to fold his ears into configurations that bear a strong resemblance to Yoda. They make me smile and laugh. If I'm a little crazy or even ridiculous, any significance that might attach is of no consequence.

I choose to believe that the meadow before the Rainbow Bridge is a *real place* and that one day I will again embrace Sabre and all the people and pets who have gone before.

Sabre's ashes reside in a carved cedar box on top of a shelf in my living room, along with the cards from friends, his picture in a frame, a small plaster cast of a German Shepherd that was a memento from EJ's collection, and a Native American bear fetish given to me by a friend to protect the house.

When the world is cold outside or too hot for comfort, when my heart is heavy, or when a dream has been trampled in the uncertainties of living, I feel, in his way, that he is still keeping me safe.

Sabre was my angel. He just happened to have a tail.

The Rainbow Bridge

By the edge of a woods, at the foot of a hill,
Is a lush, green meadow where time stands still.
Where the friends of man and woman do run,
When their time on earth is over and done.

For here, between this world and the next,
Is a place where each beloved creature finds rest.
On this golden land, they wait and they play,
Till the Rainbow Bridge they cross over one day.

No more do they suffer, in pain or in sadness,
For here they are whole, their lives filled with gladness.
Their limbs are restored, their health renewed,
Their bodies have healed, with strength imbued.

They romp through the grass, without even a care,
Until one day they start, and sniff at the air.
All ears prick forward, eyes dart front and back,
Then all of a sudden, one breaks from the pack.

For just at that instant, their eyes have met;
Together again, both person and pet.
So they run to each other, these friends from long past,
The time of their parting is over at last.

The sadness they felt while they were apart,
Has turned into joy once more in each heart.
They embrace with a love that will last forever,
And then, side by side, they cross over . . . together.

Inspired by a Norse legend, author unknown

Where We All Wait, impression by Alison Skillin (Scotland) of the meadow before the Rainbow Bridge.

Angel
With a Tail

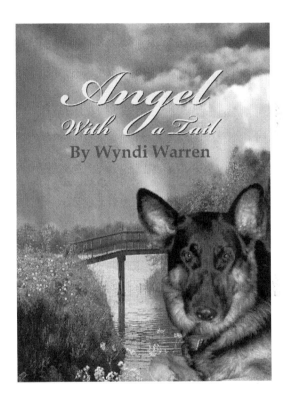

Visit www.angelwithatale.com
Write Wyndi at: AngelWithATail2011@live.com
Visit Wyn Warren on Facebook

Resources

The Degenerative Myelopathy Support Group:
http://www.mzjf.info/hgate Heaven's Gate
This is the original and foremost site for information and
support for owners of DM dogs.

The German Shepherd Dog Breed Betterment Registry:
http://www.gsdbbr.org.
This is a health registry for German Shepherds where DM is
one of the diseases that is tracked, along with a pedigree of
those dogs that have developed this disease.

**Dr, Roger Clemmons ,DVM, PhD, CVA, CVFT Former
CAPT, USPHSR, Prof of Neurology & Neurosurgery,
SACS/University of Florida:**
http://neuro.vetmed.ufl.edu/neuro/DM_Web/DMofGS.htm
The ongoing studies of Dr. Clemmons into the area of
degenerative myelopathy, a specific degenerative neurologic
disorder, has led to development of numerous therapies and
dietary supplements for treatment of the disease.

Westlab Pharmacy
4410 W. Newberry Road Suite A5
Gainesville, Florida 32607
Phone: (352) 373-8111 ~ Fax: (352) 373-8009
http://westlabpharmacy.com/animals.php?degen
Westlake specializes in compounding prescriptions and natural
products, to promote wellness.

Doggon Wheels
http://www.doggon.com/home.html
Provider of professionally used wheel chairs for dogs.
Products are used at major veterinary teaching hospitals and
physical therapy rehabilitation centers.

Eddie's Wheels
http://eddieswheels.com/
Each wheelchair is individually designed and built to your pet's
specific measurements and to address its individual needs,
incorporating the highest engineering standards with special
consideration to each pet's unique disabilities and anatomy.

HandicappedPets.com
http://handicappedpet.net/class/index.php
"HandicappedPets.com provides all of the products, services,
and support for the caretakers of disabled, injured or elderly
pets to help them enjoy healthy, happy, active lives."

Fran Smith, Vancouver, BC
howlingrainbows@yahoo.ca
Custom photo cards, photography, pottery, lanterns, whimsical
art, paintings.

Made in the USA
Charleston, SC
19 November 2011